LET ME HEAR YOUR VOICE

Portraits of Aging Immigrant Jews

Mimi E. Handlin and Marilyn Smith Layton

Photographs by **Rochelle Casserd**

UNIVERSITY OF WASHINGTON PRESS *Seattle and London*

Library of Congress Cataloging in Publication Data

Handlin, Mimi E., 1951–
　Let me hear your voice.

　1. Jews—United States—Biography.　2. United
States—Emigration and immigration—Biography.
I. Layton, Marilyn Smith, 1941–　　II. Casserd,
Rochelle.　III. Title.
E184.J5H288　1983　　973'.04924022　[B]　　83-47974
ISBN 0-295-96039-6

In loving memory of

Louis Handlin and Slava Handlin,
the father and grandmother of Mimi Handlin

Mollie and Sam Hockenberg,
the mother and father of Marilyn Smith Layton

William Stanton Wienir and Max Breetwor,
the father and grandfather of Rochelle Casserd

Acknowledgments

From the beginning of our work on *Let Me Hear Your Voice*, we have appreciated the generous support we have had from people interested in the project. For the stories told by the participants themselves, as our introduction concludes, there is no adequate word of thanks. For the University of Washington Press, whose belief in the possibility of this book was always an inspiring force in our work, we want to record our profound gratitude. For the administration and staff of the Kline Galland Home; the administration and Humanities Division of North Seattle Community College; the rabbis, cantors, and members of the Jewish community who gave us referrals; and for our friends whose encouragement kept us going, we would also like to record our deep appreciation. And to our families who most thoroughly share our pleasure in this book because they were willing to accommodate their lives as well to the commitment we made to it, we would like to express our abundant love and thanks: Rochelle's go especially to her husband Fred, her children Susan, John, and Bob, and her mother Birdye Wienir; Mimi's to her friend Bob Pilisuk and her mother Dorothy Handlin; and Marilyn's to her husband Richard, her children Larry and Eleanor, and to her mother Mollie Hockenberg, who loved listening to these stories even in the last weeks of her life.

Introduction

This is a book of stories and pictures, born of the love we had for our own immigrant grandparents and of the pleasure we have found in our teaching, social work, and photography with older people. The men and women who speak and look out from these pages have created a memorial to other times and places, and through their stories, given us precious and diverse insights into history, Judaism, cruelty, endurance, humor, and love. They have opened their homes to us and entrusted their words to our judgment.

We have been working on this book for two years, always with a sense of urgency. We wanted to preserve these stories not only for the children and grandchildren of the participants but also for those who, like ourselves, let slip the opportunity of recording similar recollections in their own families. We also wanted to preserve them for those who will never know this generation of immigrants.

The fifty men and women presented here range in age from their late sixties to one hundred, and all came to the United States before 1950. They live in a variety of places: their own homes or apartments, retirement homes, and the Jewish home for the aged. In selecting them from the larger group of those we interviewed—people we already knew, people they knew, people recommended by friends, colleagues, Rabbis, and Cantors—we sought diversity of background, country of origin, personality, and experience. We relied in our final selection on our own feelings about how the stories affected us and how they contributed to the whole of the collection.

Stories similar to these have been told in cities all over the United States where Jewish immigrants have lived. Although our participants share the circumstance of living in Seattle at the time we were working on the book, they represent a broad population of immigrants who arrived in this country during the first half of this century.

Many participants have themselves lived in other cities before coming to Seattle. A few have moved here only recently to be near their children. The exception, the Sephardic Jews, often came here directly because they had been told it was the place in this country most like their islands, Rhodes and Marmara. In thinking about the location of Seattle, one woman suggested that the aging immigrants of this city may be an unusually hearty group because they had the energy, having made the difficult journey to New York, to pick up again and travel across country in an age when such travel took nine days by train.

Of course not everyone we approached was interested in being a part of the book. One man's wife explained that nothing he could say in a page could begin to reflect the breadth of his life or his knowledge. One woman said gently on the telephone, "You won't be hurt, but remembering is not a pleasant thing for me." She continued with a bit of explanation, and then concluded sadly, "Now I am talking to you and remembering, and all of it comes back to me and follows me through the days."

Sometimes people thought they had nothing of value to contribute: "What do I have to say?" they would ask. Those whom we interviewed quickly discovered their own answers to that question. Once the process of remembering began, detail upon detail returned from the past. People occasionally called us to tell us more stories or to give us more details about something they had already said.

We did not conduct the interviews with a uniform series of questions, but rather suggested that each person begin simply talking about such matters as what they were doing at the present time, what life was like for them when they first arrived in the United States, and what they remembered from their childhood in their countries of origin. From what they told us came our questions. In this way, each interview took on a shape of its own, more easily controlled by the person speaking.

Our decision to limit each narrative to a single page involved us in an extended process of taping the interviews; transcribing all the potentially usable material, sometimes fifteen or twenty pages long; reading, rereading, and thinking about the written transcript; and, finally, choosing what we would use, listening especially for important introductory or closing statements. Sometimes a single story from the interview was so good that we used it exclusively. Other times we found it necessary to include a large swath of time and detail in order to express the essence of what someone had said.

In addition to choices about what material we would use from the interview, we also had to establish guidelines about how to reflect the oral language on the page. We kept the linguistic patterns of the original interview intact as long as they did not distort the sense of what someone was saying. The biggest obstacle in learning to speak English is its complex verb structures, particularly the auxiliaries. We noticed a tendency to use past and present tenses interchangeably, a practice which in writing sometimes works and sometimes does not. Where it did not work, we made changes.

Another difficulty in learning English is mastering its conjunctions, those squirts of glue which produce a sense of cohesiveness and flow. Again our goal has been to preserve the original statements, adding a transitional conjunction or phrase only when clarity was in question. The voice, after all, with its inflections, can create subtleties of meaning that appear intolerably choppy on the page.

With these small exceptions, we have rendered the words of these interviews as they were spoken, retaining Yiddish phrases when they did not obscure the sense of the narrative. For guidance about the language and how to transliterate it, we relied on Leo Rosten's *The Joys of Yiddish*.

After we had typed an interview in its edited form, we returned to the person whose story it was so that each participant would know exactly how the story was going to appear in the book. Sometimes the response was an addition of a phrase, or a correction or qualification of what had been said. Often the response was surprise: "I said all that?" or "You got it all down!"

In our search for an effective format, we were inspired by two books: *Number Our Days* by Barbara Myerhoff (New York: Dutton, 1978), and *After Ninety* by Imogen Cunningham (Seattle and London: University of Washington Press, 1977). In *Let Me Hear Your Voice* we hope we have succeeded in combining something of the quality of the older Jewish voices which we admired in the first book with the photographic format that engaged us in the second.

In almost every interview, we noticed the importance of photographs in the participants' lives. They often showed us their albums and took us through their homes to see the pictures of their relatives, of themselves, of family occasions, of special trips.

The photographs in this book attempt to preserve each person's individuality in the group. The expressions and gestures of the men and women were captured both during and after the interviews. Our objective was the natural image, in available light. Unaccustomed to this approach, people would smile, clasp their hands, and wait to be photographed. The camera's click at the unexpected moment surprised

them. "You took a picture? I wasn't ready!" or "You take a picture while I'm talking?"

We considered several ways of arranging these stories: by the person's place of origin, age, or date of arrival in this country, or by thematic similarities and contrasts. Each grouping had its possibilities and its problems. We decided finally upon alphabetical order because we did not want to impose any one perspective on the narratives and because no matter how they are arranged, they echo and resonate from one to the other. While each story and portrait are, like poems, complete in themselves, the stories together depict a social, cultural, and political history of Jews who came to America before 1950.

Because in our purpose and our work we have always concentrated on recording and distilling these firsthand histories, we made a deliberate decision not to create an accompanying analytic structure of our own. We leave it to others, according to their own interests, to make correlations or conclusions among the stories about history, anthropology, sociology, and gerontology. We hope that people interested in these and other related fields will find the book a valuable resource in their work.

To the question, often asked by the participants, "Why are you interested in doing such a book?" the answer that we were Jewish mattered above all others. We discovered that our authority came not from our professional experience in writing, teaching, and working with older people, but from the fact of our Judaism. From the interviews we began to gain new insight into how profoundly many of the men and women have been committed to and guided by the laws and traditions of Judaism. Their stories often testify to the courage and fortitude they have gathered from their faith.

For these immigrants, America was not so much a land of opportunity as a country of escape. The narratives are not always distinguished by the fact of their religion, yet most of them came here because they were fleeing persecution as Jews. Though some may have come for the riches America offered, many lost what they had previously had in the move—their families, their professions, their possessions, and their status. Farmers became peddlers, lawyers became bookkeepers, women with servants became workers. What has struck us is their lack of self-pity or bitterness, in spite of what they have endured. Another observation we cannot escape is that some of the people in this book are alive today because they had the courage to leave everything but their lives behind.

This book and its people have touched our own lives deeply. We have a new understanding of what we, who were born and live in the United States, have never had to face. In the participants we have new friends, whose experiences and words will continue to echo in our own. Our city looks different to us now because wherever we go, someone lives nearby. For those who have given us these stories, there is no adequate word of thanks.

Marilyn Smith Layton
Seattle, Washington
1983

Let me see your face,

Let me hear your voice,

For your voice is sweet,

And your face is comely.

—from *Song of Solomon*

Let Me Hear Your Voice

Portraits of Aging Immigrant Jews

Susan Angel

Turkey

I crossed the Atlantic three times, fourteen days each time. An agent, a Sephardic Jew named Hannanell, had sent us over the first time. He made a thousand dollars on us.

My mother, my sister, and I were coming because my father was here already as a Rabbi with my older brothers. We left Istanbul in June 1921. We came to Ellis Island and were there fourteen days, incarcerated. I was so awed to see the place, a huge building surrounded by wire fence. We could not get out. We were only waiting for my dad to send tickets.

In the meantime, my mother was crying every day. We were anxious why we hadn't heard from my dad. On the fourteenth day, they called us on the loudspeakers by our names, but we couldn't understand either the Russian or the English. They had to bring a Sephardic interpreter in. The interpreter gathered us around and said in Ladino, "We are very sorry but your agent in Istanbul should have told you that the quota in New York was full, and they will not let you into America. You will have to go back." I will always remember that moment. Everybody was crying, pulling their hair. My mother said, "How can I notify my husband? He's in Seattle, Washington." We didn't even know where Seattle was.

It took us all day to pack up our things to go back. We got on the boat the same afternoon, and they put each of us in a separate cabin or cage. I was in a cage with the rest, all young Russian ladies, with a wire fence around the outside. Maybe they thought I would jump. To this day I don't know how to swim.

I didn't know where my mother or sister was. I was screaming, screaming to God to hear me. The Russian ladies were screaming more. I heard the ship's toot-toot. They pulled up the anchor and we left. We didn't even see the harbor. All we saw was the lady, the Statue of Liberty, but we didn't know what she was or who she was at the time.

We went about a half an hour, still crying and screaming; then all of a sudden I hear, "Victoria Azose! Victoria Azose!" When the sailors saw we could not jump overboard, they opened the cage and asked, "Who is Susan Azose?" I said, "Me, me, me!" They pulled me out, grabbed me by the arm. "Who is Victoria?" "Mama, Mama," I'm telling them. They went and got my mother and sister, and they showed us the telegram my father had sent. It was in Spanish. It said: "Dear Simcha:" (Simcha was her name before

she got very sick and they changed it to Vida in Spanish, meaning life, Victoria in English.) "Don't worry. Have patience. God will be with you three, and, God willing, I will try again next year to send you some more money for more tickets. Rev. Izak Azose."

We got back to Istanbul and our agent, that rat Hannanell who had sent us over, met us with a fancy buggy. He told us that he was very sorry, that he thought once we were in America, because we were a Rabbi's family, they would let us in and not send us back. He did not give us back our thousand dollars, but he took us to a hotel in Serkiji, a fancy suburb across the bridge from Istanbul. At the hotel we had breakfast, lunch, and dinner, all kosher, for a whole week till we told him to get in touch with our brother. To make amends, Hannanell paid for it all. We stayed with my brother and his wife almost a year because we had sold everything, our home, our furniture, before we left.

One day we received a special-delivery letter from America—a letter from America was like seeing the face of God—and it had money. My father had sent a letter to another agent telling him to make new tickets for us. We left the end of June 1922. We arrived in Ellis Island a second time but were there just three days. We got a letter from my father with the tickets for the train and you wouldn't believe, if you looked at our faces, how joyful, how happy we were. On the third day, they opened the gates, let us into New York, and I swear I still don't know how we got from Ellis Island to the train, we were so excited.

We got on the train, and it took us five days to Seattle. One evening in the middle of the road, we saw lights, shooting sparkles. I got scared because in Turkey they used to tell me, "When you go to America, you're going to find Indians, and they shoot arrows, and they're going to kill you." I was so scared I ran to my mother and sister and tried to hide from the Indians. I didn't understand it was the Fourth of July.

I raised seven children, worked in a suitcase factory for many years, and now like to work at the Jewish home for the aged. I like to take care of the people. I talk to them, sing to them, play with them cards, take them for walks, cut their food and feed them if they need it, and help out on days when everybody is supposed to tell their story how they came from the old country.

Regina Avzaradel

Isle of Rhodes

I don't know the year I was born because they never registered it. Our parents used to write it in a book and that's all. I come from the Isle of Rhodes. I lived there until 1916. When I was there, we didn't have anything ready-made. We couldn't buy anything. We didn't have electric lights or running water. We used to cook, bake, and sew at home for the men and for the children. We had to go outside and walk so many blocks away to get the water. But we had a lot of fun. We were happy.

The Jews were very religious. We would get together for the holidays, singing and dancing. We used to call ourselves a small Israel and that was before Israel was born.

In 1916 I left for America to get married. We used to get married by pictures. My mother-in-law liked me and said, "I'll give you my son for a husband." He was in America, so I sent him a picture and he sent me a picture and then he sent me money to go to him in Atlanta, Georgia. On the boat some people said, "Who are you going to see in America? Relatives?"

I said, "I got nobody except my fiancé and I never saw him before."

They said, "Suppose you go there and you don't like him. What are you going to do?"

I went to bed that night and couldn't sleep, thinking what if he saw me and told me, "I don't want you." Where could I go? I don't know nobody. I don't know even the language. He met me at the boat and took me to a place where I could board. After three months, we got married.

In 1920 we went back to the Isle of Rhodes, stayed there a year, and then came back to America to North Carolina. It was a beautiful place. They called it the Land of the Sky. At night you could put out your hand and reach the stars. Then we came to Seattle.

We never had any children but I got one anyway. I adopted her when she was ten months old. I wouldn't take a million dollars for her. Now she's got two of her own and that's my family. My husband passed away.

I've been here in the Jewish home for almost two years. It's a beautiful place. There is a patio where I can sit if I want to go outside, and in the wintertime, you can see the lake through the trees.

Louise Azose

Turkey

They needed a Rabbi very badly in Seattle so my father came with mother and the younger children. My sister and I stayed in Turkey because of the quota. She was already eighteen. With a Rabbi for a father, it's just what your father tells you—no dates, no going out. It was just terrible. I was about fifteen when my father and mother came to America, and I was very active. So when he left, I said, "Now's my time."

Two and a half years later, my sister and I came to Vancouver, British Columbia, worse than dirty at the time. Somebody made the papers for us, like we had a sister in Vancouver which we didn't. The train from Halifax to Vancouver took eight, nine nights. No planes then. My sister and I got tired and sick. Quiet, quiet, quiet, me and my sister. A man gave us a bunch of bananas. I thought it was poison he was giving us. I said to my sister, "It's poison. Don't touch them."

Always in doubt. Always. That's why I was so afraid on the train. Till I came to America. Till I married my husband. Always in doubt. Peddlers coming to sell something—I thought, "That's it. They come to get us."

We were in Vancouver about nine months. In the meantime, my father was making papers for us to come to the United States. He went to the immigration office and got a pass for me to come here for four months.

My husband had a sister I met when I came to Seattle. He came to his mother's house and said, "Where's my sister?" She said, "She's with a girl from Vancouver at a show." So he left his meal—he didn't want to eat—and he came over and sat behind us in the movie, his sister and myself. He saw me and he said, "That's for me. That's it."

My time was up. I had to go back to Vancouver, so we got engaged. He couldn't stand it without me. First love. He came over to Vancouver and said, "Honey, I can't stand it. I have to do something." He became a citizen right away so he could bring me over. That day he had off and came to Vancouver. We went to the license people. They said, "You can't go just with the license to the United States. You have to be married." I said, "My God, we're Jewish people. We have to get married by Rabbis." My father was a Rabbi, his father was a Rabbi. We didn't know what to do.

We finally said, "Where can we find a church?" They said Wesley Church was the best in Vancouver. We went in. I'm so afraid, being in a church. I'm a Jewish girl. What's she doing in a church? I just wanted to run away. My husband said, "Honey, don't worry. Everything is going to be okay." We went in and he called a witness. The preacher was there, and he started with the Holy Ghost. Then he said, "Where is your ring?" My husband went and got a ring for ten cents and we got married.

When we got back to Seattle, he had to go to his father's house, I had to go to my father's house. We only told our parents that we had been married. Nine months later, we got married again, in the synagogue.

The day that I was going to get married, I got sick from excitement. I told my father. Then you had to tell everything to the father. My husband was working for Ford and they gave him a week vacation. He was all ready. But my father said, "I'm sorry, Louise, you can't go on your honeymoon. You have to stay with us and he has to go home." I said, "What's that? We have to go. His week is on!" My husband was furious. I said, "Honey, that's my father." I'm talking about fifty-four years ago. You had to do what your father said. My father said, "Unless you take a chaperone with you." My husband's sister was ready. She said, "Louise, I'm going with you if you want me. I'm going to sleep in the middle." So that's what we did, so help me God. We took my husband's new Ford and my sister-in-law, and we went to a hotel, and she slept in the middle.

Never in my life did I work. I didn't have to. Right away I had kids. How can you work? Never time. At home plenty. One day my sister-in-law said, "Why don't you come with me?" She worked in a suitcase factory. "Work, just for fun." She took me over there with her. I started on the machine. I didn't like it but I did it. When I came home, I was so tired, the whole day working there. My kids, my husband, they say, "Mom, don't cook dinner. We'll take you out." They did. They served me like a queen. One day in my life and I said, "No more."

I'm seventy-five. They ask me, "To the same man you're married fifty-four years?" I say, "Yes, I don't want to change."

Annemarie Ballin

Germany

The human being is very adaptable. You get used to a lot of things. And I was young at the time, and a born optimist. It is so long ago it is as if it happened in another life. They took away the stores, they took away the houses, they could throw you out of an apartment because you were Jewish. We had in our passports, "Israel." My husband was not anymore a physician, he was a "treater of the sick." Who dreamed up these things, I don't know, just to make life miserable.

The worst time was what they called Crystal Night. They tore down the synagogue in Munich where we lived and made a parking lot. They arrested all the Jewish men in order, according to the alphabet. They came to our house at five in the morning and arrested my husband. We didn't know where the men were. They put him in Dachau for two days. He was lucky because he was the last Jewish gynecologist in the Jewish Hospital in Munich, and one of his patients expected a baby. They let him out.

We had been planning to emigrate, but I got polio in 1937, and that, of course, made an end to our emigration for the moment. Some relatives in the United States gave an affidavit to my husband. I would have needed a very high affidavit, but with the husband there, they usually let the wife come. My husband left Germany in March 1939, and took our daughter, ten years old, to England and left her there in Cambridge with an English Jewish family. Half a year later, the war broke out and there we were.

When I finally got my visa, I had to take a train from Munich to Genoa, Italy. A Jewish girl from Munich traveled with me because I couldn't travel alone. The trains had very high steps so I had my trunk go through duty before. It was sealed so that I wouldn't have to get out at the border. One of the SS men came through the train and said, "Everybody has to get out at the Austria-Italian border." (Austria was already Germany.) I said, "I can't get out." He said, "You have to."

The train got to the border. There were flowers, it was decorated, but the train didn't stop. In Milan, Italian soldiers came into the train. A soldier who could speak a little German said, "Hitler and Mussolini just met." That's why the train didn't stop, and why we didn't have to get off.

One misconception people have is that you couldn't leave Germany. You could always get out if you didn't take anything with you. You just couldn't get into other countries without visas. My family was killed— my mother, my sister, the whole family—in Auschwitz. I had no affidavits for them.

When I came to the United States in April 1940, the situation in Germany was so bad that we thought everything here was wonderful. We were together again. A half year later, we got our daughter out of England. She came on the last children's transport. We had one room in New York, a sublet from another refugee family, and I had kitchen privileges. The trouble was I couldn't cook. In Germany, the middle class had live-in maids.

My husband had to study and I had to work. He passed his state boards in Massachusetts, and we moved first to a small place near Worcester. I still remember the first night. It was in summer, in August. We went outside. It was a beautiful summer night, hot in the yard, and I thought to myself, "Never forget this moment." It was a new start. The family was together again.

All my life I had lived in a big city—first Berlin, then Munich—and I didn't adjust very well in that small town. My poor daughter was twelve years old then. I took the standards I was used to and they didn't quite fit here, but I didn't see it. One day she wanted to go to Worcester to a movie and afterwards to a drugstore. I let her go to the movie, but after the movie, she had to come right home. A very harmless thing to get a soft drink, but I just didn't know, and I didn't have anyone to talk to whose standards I would have accepted.

When I came here, I thought I was a good democrat—with a little *d*. I found that was not true. I thought on Sunday in Germany when my maid had a day off, I was very nice to wash the dishes. We had really no idea. In Germany, there was a big separation in the social strata. This, I thought, is the wonderful thing here, how quickly you can advance from one level to the next. I never quite got over it.

One day we went to the opera. My husband parked the car and he said, "Guess whom I met. The vegetable man from Safeway, dressed fit to kill, with his wife at the opera!"

When my husband died, my physician knew I was looking for something to do and he got me an interview at an organization where they train handicapped people for jobs. A woman interviewed me. I said I had no skills and then I thought about Braille, which I had learned years before. Now I transcribe books into Braille. It's something what was needed, and it keeps me busy. You know, that was my salvation.

Margit Baruch

Hungary and Austria

Before I was born, my parents had lost two of their three children. There was only my one sister left, and all my parents could think of was they wanted another child. Then the miracle happened. I came in 1905. I was the spoildest baby in the whole world. It was a wonderful growing-up.

The city in Hungary where we lived, Kecskemet, grew the most beautiful fruit. The apricots and peaches and plums I can still see in my dreams. We had a beautiful big house with a cook and a maid. My parents were both highly intelligent. My father taught me everything. He and his friends would sit around the table with political and intellectual discussions and I, at the age of seven, didn't have the faintest idea what they were talking about. Then all of a sudden, a voice would say, "Margit, did you understand what I said?" I would say, "Huh?" Then my father would say, "Would you kindly speak properly?"

"No, I didn't understand because I didn't listen."

"If we are speaking, you have to listen, and if you don't understand you have to ask."

That kind of craziness helped me grow up the way I am, a highly political animal. And I was always spoiled. I was still that way when Hitler came. I wouldn't take no for an answer, so nothing happened to me. Seventy of my family were killed, so it wasn't easy. But I, personally, must have had six guardian angels around me because otherwise how could I do what I did and get away with it?

I had moved from Hungary to Vienna and was living there in 1938 when Hitler came. I had my own store where I sold raw and baked and roasted poultry. I was also deeply involved in politics. We were supposed to have a plebiscite to decide, "No, we don't want Hitler to take over Austria." When customers came into my store, I screamed at them, "You are going to vote on Sunday for heaven's sake, don't forget to vote." I didn't know who were Nazis. I stuck my neck out. You have to know how afraid you are and how much you want to risk. On Saturday before the election, the newspaper came out and there was a big article saying Hitler should come, so the voting was 99.8 percent for Hitler. When the Hitler people came, gentiles could not enter a Jewish store and, of course, the situation became terrible.

My name was a very good name. I wrote letters to England and America and everywhere: "My name is Baruch. Help." Slowly but surely the different Jewish committees helped. In London, you could go as a maid. We had always had a cook and a maid so I never cleaned house. I had never even been in a kitchen. My father wouldn't let me. He didn't like the smell of food cooking. So I went to a school where Jewish business women were taught to be maids. I got a job in London.

The Hitler people couldn't give me a passport though, because they thought there must still be money somewhere. So I went to the passport office and said, "What lousy Nazis are you? Are you not ashamed of yourselves? Your Führer wants the Jews out, I want to go out, I have a job to go to, the Jewish Committee is paying my fare and you won't put that lousy stamp on my passport? Shame on you." They stamped the passport and I left for London on Passover, 1939. My guardian angels were with me. I worked for an old Jewish family there, scrubbing floors and cooking.

In Seattle was a German priest who brought many refugees over, including my sister and brother-in-law. In 1946 my sister sent for me. I worked at Sears, Roebuck and Company until I retired in 1967.

I am still involved in politics. I tell people to know what they are voting for. Since I lived under Hitler, I know where it can lead if you don't know what you are doing. I'm highly successful in all the things I do because I'm stronger than anybody and I don't give up. People say to me, "How do you do it?" All I can say is, "I don't know. Somehow or another, it's done."

Henry Benezra

Turkey

I'm a man from another century, born in 1899. Turkey was a tolerant country because it had a *millet* system. Every ethnic group had its own representatives in the government. Each group lived in their own quarters and had the freedom to use their own language, their own newspapers, their own schools. We were a poor family and lived in the Turkish section in Istanbul.

I grew up in a matriarchal household. My father was incapacitated so my mother was working. She worked for the Singer Sewing Machine Company in Turkey. Some of the nobility would buy sewing machines and my mother would teach the women in the harems how to run the machines. Men were not allowed in the harems, but when I was a little boy, my mother would take me with her. I had the opportunity to see all kinds of women in the different households. Turkish Orthodox women, English ladies, Italian ladies—all married to noble Turks.

I started school in the Talmud Torah. After three or four years, I wanted to change schools so I went to the French Jewish school, the Alliance Israelite Universelle. It was a different culture there. No one spoke Ladino, so I had to learn French. After a few months, I went to a German school, the Hilfsverein der Deutschen Juden. This school was a different setup because it was multilingual. The teachers couldn't understand each other. I had a Turkish class, a French class, a German class, and a Hebrew class. The Hebrew class was the most important to me. I knew the liturgy, but conversational Hebrew was something different.

I didn't finish school in Turkey because in 1908 there was a revolution. The Turkish college students were rebelling against the autocratic form of government and decided to overthrow the king, Abdul Hamid. At that time, I was still a young child and I could hear rumblings at night, shouting and shooting. My father was education minded and he would take me with him to see what's going on. On Saturday mornings, there was a tradition among the elder men that they would get up before daybreak and go to the different people's houses and chant devotional hymns.

My father would take me with him in the dark. After they would read a little bit, the men would drink coffee and talk about current events. That gave me quite a bit of insight into what was going on.

It was interesting, because although the idea of freedom sounded good, we were a very protected society. Everyone had their own schools, their own language, their own courts. When the freedom movement came along, they nationalized the secular schools and put emphasis on the Turkish language. All of this was new to the people who didn't know the Turkish customs or religion. The army was completely Moslem, but after the revolution they said, "We are all one in the fighting for the fatherland, whether you are Greek or Jew or Turk." As an edict, they started drafting people who were not Moslem. People could pay an exemption to get out of the army, but only the well-to-do could afford it.

There was an exodus. Many people tried to leave, because they couldn't merge with the culture and the draft was terrible. Besides, there were rumblings of war. My mother didn't like the idea of the draft. I had four brothers. My oldest brother left first, and then one at a time all the brothers went to America. I also had two sisters. One went to America and one went to Bulgaria. Finally only I, the youngest, was left with my parents. In August 1911, we all came to the United States.

When I remember my childhood in Turkey, it was the cultural part that impressed me the most. Such a tremendous country, full of history. I was lucky to be exposed to so many different cultures and people. I had firsthand information, nothing from hearsay. What more could I want? I do a lot of reading and I like to reminisce. I'm trying to capture my experiences with the different cultures and languages in writing. I feel a responsibility to write. I'm wondering why my mind runs in that direction. Maybe it goes back to Rabbi Benezra, the Hebrew poet. Then there was Moses Benezra, the Hebrew poet. Maybe some of their genes came down to me.

Dona Benoun

Turkey

We came from Turkey. That's why my broken English. We lived a lot of different places. I used to go to Istanbul two times a month. We went by boat. Three hours and we would be there, lovely, beautiful . . . but still I tell you, America is America. When we didn't know America, Istanbul was number one. But now, here is number one.

When World War I came, my father decided to come to America to save the family. The Turkish army wanted to take my brothers to be soldiers. We came here to America, three brothers, my mother, father, and myself. My oldest brother came here first because of the war. They were going to draft him. Another brother was already drafted and wore a uniform, but my father knew people in the court who taught him how to take my brother from the service. We all came on the boat and my brother, in uniform, came inside the boat to see us off. But he stayed and hid inside the boat. He went into the bathroom and took off his uniform. We brought other clothes for him and threw away his uniform in the sea in the middle of the night.

We got to Seattle in 1919. My older brother, already there, had prepared a nice home for us and I got engaged right away. How I met my husband is another story. One of my friends from the old country wanted me to go to a show with her. We didn't drive, we didn't take a bus, we walked. My husband had a fruit stand down on Yesler Way. My friend said, "Let's buy something and we'll eat it at the show." My husband was hanging a bunch of bananas and started asking me all kind of questions. "When did you come here? How many brothers do you have?" Somehow he found out about our family coming here and wanted to see if I was from that family. How he found out, I don't know. He gave us a big bunch of cherries and said, "I want to give you a present because you people, you just came to America." I took the fruit, said, "Thank you, good-bye," and we went to the show.

Well, he kept it in his mind and told his cousin all about me. He said, "That girl is for me. You are going to do something before somebody else comes to take her." We only met one time, so help me God.

His cousin came to me and said, "Do you remember the man who gave you the cherries?"

I said, "Yes, you mean the Greek?" I thought he was Greek because he had a mustache.

"No, he is Jewish, Sephardim. Do you want to come to my house and meet him?" she asked.

I said, "Why are you rushing me? I know nothing!"

But they did it. They fixed it and I got engaged and three months later, married. We had a happy marriage because he was a good man. I was lucky. We had three daughters and a son, a big family. Now I have eleven grandchildren and seven great-grandchildren.

I had a nice time. I used to cook, go to my friends. I knew how to manage. Everything was fine.

Now I am here in the home because I couldn't stay alone in my house. My children wanted to help, but I don't want to bother nobody. I have been here almost four years. I know the day is going to come . . . someday I'm going to die. The only thing is, I hope to God not to let me suffer. If he wants it, I'm going to go. From the beginning I'm happy, proud that I am Jewish.

The Jewish people, they believe in God. In the old country, everybody was religious and still I am the same. I am an old lady. It doesn't pay to change. I accept life. That's all. The way I grew up, the way I am, the same way I'm going to die.

Nicholas Berman

Hungary

I am very grateful to America, but I don't feel so much American. An American born here can criticize the government, but if it happens I am criticizing, someone can say, "Then why did you come here?" I don't feel completely at home, and I go back to Hungary or Czechoslovakia, and I don't feel at home. To my city where I was born, I don't want to go back. My city is in Russia now.

When I was born, in 1909, Uzhored was part of the Austria-Hungarian monarchy. I had a beautiful childhood, the seventh of eight children with good and understanding parents. School went easily without any trouble and I had excellent friends. I didn't know what was suffering. After *Gymnasium*, I went on to medical school in Prague. I finished in 1934 when Hitler was already in power in Germany.

My experiences after that, I don't think too much about. People hear what I and others went through, and they say, "How could they do it?"—to see and experience such terrible things. But when comes the time, you have to do it. After a while, you don't feel the pain.

In 1941 I was taken into forced labor to work for a medical corps attached to the German army. The Germans were fighting the Russians in Poland, and we had to treat the German soldiers. It was there I saw the worst brutality to the Jewish people. They were lined up by big ditches and a special SS group massacred them with machine guns. I couldn't say anything.

During that time, the officers in the medical unit were afraid we would be attacked by partisans during the night. They told me, as a good ambassador, to go out and speak to the people and let them know that we were a medical unit, not a fighting unit. One day I went to a house. The German soldiers stayed outside, and a big red-haired man answered the door. He looked like a Russian. I went in and told him my story about the unit and I also told him that I was a Jew. He asked me how come I was with the Germans, and I told him that twelve Jewish physicians were forced into the German army. He looked at me a long time and then came in front of me and very slowly and very quietly said, "Shema Yisrael," and I answered him, "Adonoi Elohenu." When I remember this moment, I want to cry. He embraced me and kissed my cheek, filled with happiness to see another Jew. He just opened himself up. I could have been an *agent provocateur*.

In 1942–43 I was free and living with my wife in my home town. By then the Germans were occupying Hungary and, like the other countries they occupied, they decided to kill all the Jews. They forced all the Jewish people into a brick factory to stay. There were about fifteen thousand of us. The degradation was terrible. Among us, people were defecating on the ground, young people were making love. They took every day three thousand or five thousand people on the train, and we didn't know where they were going. We were the last to go, in a cattle boxcar with eighty people.

Three days and three nights to Auschwitz, with no sanitation and no water. There were many old people and they looked to me, as a doctor, to help them. When we got to Auschwitz, the famous Dr. Mengele selected people to the left and to the right. Out of three thousand people about three hundred were selected to live. My wife and I were among them because we looked strong. The human being is very adaptable. You break in very fast. I recall when I was carrying friends of mine, removing dead bodies for six or seven hours. At the beginning it was terrible, but after awhile I became frozen. I was in the camps until May 1945.

After we were freed, my wife found me. I was in a hospital and weighed less than a hundred pounds. There were only three couples from our whole town who found each other. When you are in the camps, you only think you have given up all hope. But it's still there inside. When I saw my wife, I was filled with hope to meet the other members of my family. Finally you realize the truth and then comes the depression. It happened to everybody.

I started a new life in Czechoslovakia to practice medicine again. I was relatively happy, but it was very difficult to get back. You become so callous, no feeling. The only feeling is a certain kind of hatred and you have to get rid of it. You cannot live with it, especially to be a doctor and take care of people. Gradually, I accommodated. It was easier for us because we had each other.

We came to the United States in 1946 because the Russians wanted to force me to practice medicine in Russia. When we got here, it was very difficult, learning how to read, write, and speak the language, going to school, taking the medical boards. But I had wonderful friends wherever I went. I want to leave the past behind me. Thank God, since we came to this country, life has been good to me.

Z. William Birnbaum

Poland

When I first arrived in the United States in 1937, I was thirty-three, a young man. I had completed my studies in Europe, a law degree and my doctorate in mathematics.

In Poland I had the good luck that a cousin of mine was editor-in-chief of the leading Polish newspaper. He gave me the job of a correspondent in the United States because the Polish quota was booked for decades ahead. As a journalist, I immediately got my visitor's visa, arrived in the United States, and very gently wrote my reports. Meanwhile in New York, one of my former professors from Göttingen, who had had to leave Germany, gave me my first paying position in the United States, a research position at New York University. That was the beginning of my academic career here.

One of my first impressions of what this country stands for was about three days after I had arrived in New York. I walked over to Columbus Circle and there was a cluster of people surrounding what I later learned was called a soap box, and on that soap box stood a man gesturing rather violently, calling President Roosevelt all kinds of names—a lesson in the American vernacular worth the price of admission.

In Poland about a year before I left, a statute was enacted that established a new criminal offense. The offense was "Insult to the Polish State," so vaguely defined that if somebody told a streetcar conductor, a government official after all, that he was a louse, that was enough to be charged with an insult to the state, pulled before a judge, and locked up for several months.

Now there was that man on the soap box insulting the president of the United States. I stood there and waited for a policeman to show up and haul him away, and it happened. A policeman came by. A huge guy, red faced, no expression. He stood there, got closer, played yo-yo with his nightstick, watched the events going on. Then instead of doing what I thought he should, he turned on his heel and spit. He spit farther than I ever knew a person could spit. And that was the end of it. And that was my first lesson in what this country stands for.

There was a counterpart to that lesson. Many years later at the University of Washington, there was a loyalty oath issue. The state legislature passed a law in the last phase of a session when nobody knew anymore what they were voting for, a completely valid statute saying that faculty members must take a loyalty oath which was spelled out completely.

That thing hit me rather hard. A group of faculty members filed suit to declare that law unconstitutional, and I was one of them. That summer I was invited to the Polish Academy of Sciences for a lecture circuit with the academy. In order to meet the schedule, I had to leave before the hearings on that lawsuit. My testimony was taken by deposition, I explained my position, and my wife and I left for Poland.

When we arrived in Poland, for some reason the story of the lawsuit preceded us, and wherever we arrived, one of the first questions when we got together on a social level was, "And you are suing the state?" And the answer was yes.

One person in particular was a classmate of mine from the days before I left Poland, a prominent mathematician in Poland, a man who became very active in the Communist party. There were six or seven of us sitting around a table one day sipping something, and the question was asked again—"And you are suing the state?" And then the following conversation:

"And you mean to say you sue the state and they give you a passport?"

"Yes, obviously."

"And they let you go back?"

"Yes, I don't expect any difficulties."

"And you will be teaching again?"

"Yes, the suit is progressing. It may be years before it is finally decided. Meanwhile, there is an injunction; the law cannot be enforced."

"And you mean there will be no reprisals whatsoever? You will be drawing a salary, teaching students?"

"Yes."

And then that man, that mathematician turned politician, was silent a few seconds, then shook his head and said, "That couldn't happen here."

Somehow those two episodes—the soap box and the lawsuit, which made its way to the Supreme Court where they found the loyalty oath statute unconstitutional—illustrate to me that our country is a very good society.

As a professor emeritus now of Mathematics and Statistics, I still continue to work. I was not pleased to have to retire because I had to stop teaching, but the other things I am interested in can be continued—my research, my publications work, and my consulting. One thing I would not want to do is sit in front of a television set and wait.

Tamara Birulin

Russia and China

We were three children, I and my sister and brother. My parents brought us by train as infants in 1905 from Siberia to Manchuria. They were running away from the pogroms. After a few years we moved from Manchuria to Harbin. Jewish life there was wonderful. They had a Jewish hospital and a synagogue. In Harbin, I got my education in Hebrew school and in the Jewish *Gymnasium*. After high school, I went to the university for dentistry. In 1920 I graduated. I met my husband, a pharmacist, and we married. We moved to Tientsin where my husband and father got a job. In 1921 I got my oldest son in Tientsin. Eight years later, I got my youngest son.

China was paradise—in all life, in all the reasons. I had four servants: a cook, *amah* (like a nanny), a coolie who did the dirty work, and a boy who delivered the food.

I was the oldest in the family. My brother and sister returned to Russia to go to the university. All of a sudden, Russia stopped the communication. We never saw them again. Once it happened though that a dentist came to Tientsin. Somebody had sent him to the Birulin family. All of a sudden he looked at my piano, seeing my sister's picture. So he says, "How come she is here?" I come up to him and say, "How you know her?" And he says, "When I was running away from Russia, I became sick and she was my doctor." And I say, "Yes, she was a doctor."

We ran away from Tientsin because the Japanese were taking over. In China, practically all the Jews came from Russia. When China began to have troubles, everyone ran away again, some back to Russia, some to Israel, some to the United States. We came here in 1940. January 11. My father's brother lived in Seattle. He sent us an affidavit.

Running away from China, we lost everything. We left a beautiful life. I never can forget it. I didn't know how to cook. At first, my soup I made from the can. Pea soup. So my son, my youngest, about ten years old, said, "Momma, it's so good! How you made it?"

The first time I had to take the garbage out, I opened the door. Someone was coming so I put the garbage down. It wasn't nice for a lady to take the garbage out. The next time, someone was coming again, so I went and put the garbage on the window. Afterwards, I took it from the window on the outside and put it out like a lady.

Now I'm not afraid to put the garbage out.

When we came here, I worked in a factory. I never saw a power machine before and I sewed my finger. My husband cried. He said, "You'll never work up there." But the floor lady came up to the foreman and said, "Tamara is crying because she broke the needle." The foreman brought me one hundred needles so I wouldn't be afraid to break them.

They learned me on the power machine. I started to sew. All of a sudden, I became a big shot, and by this time, I learn the other girls when they come. For twenty-six years I worked in the same place, making pockets in suitcases.

My older son graduated grammar school in Tientsin. Every year they still have a reunion, all around the world. This year someone said to him, "I remember your mother. She had beautiful hair and was always singing on stage." In China I studied to train my voice. All my life I was singing and playing for charity, sometimes in Russian, sometimes in Hebrew, sometimes in Jewish. My grandfather, a Rabbi, was musical too. He taught me lots of songs, even "Ave Maria" in Italian, because he liked the music. Lots of songs I know. I wish I still had the voice.

I became a citizen here several years after we came. The judge asked if I would bear arms for the United States. I thought, "Arms is arms." He meant guns. I say, "I don't think I'm understanding you." So he says it again. I still don't understand. So he says, "Are you going to protect the United States?" And then I understand. I say, "Sure! Sure!" And here I am still.

Edith Blumenfeld

Germany

Hamburg was the last city Hitler put his foot in. My husband was in a concentration camp for seven weeks, and seven weeks seemed like seven years. I'm still not sure why he got out. When he was released, we decided to emigrate. We had two children so it was not easy to go to another country. We tried to go to Israel but they wouldn't take us. My husband was too old. Then we tried Australia, but they wouldn't take us either. It was so terrible—we couldn't get a visa. Finally, we found some people in America who gave us affidavits. My parents didn't want to emigrate. They wouldn't tell us the reason, but I think they were afraid they would be a burden on us. That wasn't the case at all. They stayed. They went to Auschwitz.

Immigrating was not too hard for me. I thought it was interesting. And we were so happy in America, from the first moment when the bell rang and we knew it was not a Nazi to take us away. We lived in New York for two and a half years. Then we came to Seattle because we had met a woman years before who said Seattle was the only place to live.

I worked very hard in America. My best job was in a service station, pumping gas and lubricating cars. I loved it, all that time outside. I also worked as a cleaning woman for years. I had a job in the morning and a job in the afternoon, and then I had to rush home because the kids were coming. The job I hated was working in an office, typing and bookkeeping. I really hated it. I'd rather scrub floors. And I was working a year in a pawn shop on Skid Road. You couldn't imagine who came in there. Actually the prostitutes were quite nice, but it was dangerous. I was robbed once. My husband also had a lot of funny jobs. First he was a truck driver and then he was a checker at the Port of Seattle. They were odd jobs, not refined, but he was happy too.

I like to go to school and take French classes. I also swim, walk, and hike in the summer. There are other people eighty years old to hike in the mountains with. Being retired is like vacations in school. You can do what you want. Of course, it would be much nicer if my husband were alive, but what can I do? I still enjoy life.

Joseph Brown (born Bronshtane)

Russia

Lately I can feel the chase of the *Malach Hamoves*, the Angel of Death, that he is gaining on me. In a race with him one always comes in second best. If the dark angel obliged me with a pink slip, these would be my last thoughts: It is too late to dwell on life's disappointments, or to express regrets of things left undone. I have procrastinated so that I won't be able to read *War and Peace* cover to cover, or *Decline and Fall of the Roman Empire*, or *Das Kapital*. My aspirations have dwindled—I have in mind just three—and two of these are practically beyond my reach.

Since the age of thirteen, I've had a large musical composition in my mind. I get some small comfort from it in that I can visualize it, note by note. I don't think I have the tools to write it. Instead I satisfy my need for music now by playing my violin with the Musicians' Emeritus Orchestra.

For years I didn't play. In 1935, when I was twenty-three years old, I lost four fingers and part of the thumb of my right hand in an accident in a machine in the factory where I worked in Detroit. Even now I recoil at the gruesome details. Not the physical pain, but the memory of the shrieking siren of the ambulance and me moaning, "My poor mother, my poor mother." She was profoundly understanding of how important music was to me. While I was recuperating in the hospital, she hid my violin so that I would not constantly be reminded that I could no longer think of becoming a professional violinist.

Another unlikely desire is visiting my birthplace, Rizhin. Why do I yearn to see a remote *shtetl* in the Ukraine? Not to recall the terrible poverty my mother and we six children endured there. And surely not to witness the present suppression in that unhappy regime. Rather that I might again trod the ground, barefooted, in spring; explore the forest, with its abundance of nut trees and berries; savor fruit, usually filched from a kulak's orchard; glide on the frozen lake, a free spirit, on skates my brother Avrom made for me out of wooden slats with iron runners.

Anyone who lives long enough develops a philosophy. Mine lies with my Judaism. Oneness is the heart of Jewishness since the time of Abraham. Even if infinitesimally, I feel at one with him. I was born a Jew. I've tried to live as a Jew. I beseech Providence to fulfill my third ambition—to die as a Jew, with the Shema as my last words on my deathbed.

Sema Calvo

Isle of Marmara

I want to tell my story. I want my grandchildren to know what it means to come from another country, and how I appreciate this country.

My father came here first in 1902 to get rich. After a few years, he went back to Turkey to get married. He had two children, and my mother was pregnant with a third when he left again. Either she was coming over or he was coming back after he got richer. Then war was declared and we stayed alone for eight years. For eight years he couldn't send money, he couldn't come, we couldn't come.

Where we lived was an island, the most beautiful spot in the world, but during the war, pretty soon, there was no food. On the beach we'd see a boat coming and say, "There's going to be food." Then the Germans would bomb it, and you'd see everything going to pieces. When there was bread, my grandfather used to wait two to three hours in line for it. Very, very poor living.

When the war was over, my father sent us money to come to America. We came in steerage, four weeks just to cross. We went to Ellis Island and had butter for the first time in our lives, and white bread, and milk. We were there Rosh Hashanah, and arrived in Seattle where my father was on Yom Kippur Day. My father was so religious that he would not leave the synagogue to come and meet us at the train. He sent my uncle with a cab. That evening after the services were over, we met him for the first time in eight years. I was ten and a half.

A year and a half after we were there, he got a sleeping sickness so I had to quit school to take care of my baby brother, just a few months old, at night at my aunt's house, and to work during the day. I used to go to school half a day a week, and I got a diploma from grammar school. That's all the education I had.

I was fifteen. The boys were looking for a wife. It wasn't like now. My mother came one day and she said to my husband, "You know, there's two men after Sema, and if you don't want her, I'm going to get her engaged to one of the other guys." He said, "Yeah, okay, I'll take her!" We were engaged two and a half years.

We had a wedding for a week. When we went to pay the grocer, my husband said, "It can't be we used

ten gallons of oil." It used to be people coming and going all the week. When we got married, for eight days, you cannot leave the bride and groom alone. They only sleep together the first night. After that I slept with my aunt in the bed, and my husband in the other bed, and every night he used to say to her, "Will you please go home? I'm married! Why can't I sleep with her?" But the eating and the partying and the dancing went on for a week. A week of crazy. And that's why we used ten gallons of oil. This was how we did it in the old country and this is the way we still do.

We went four years ago back to the Isle of Marmara for the first time. Before that it had been a military base. My husband's house was still standing, but the other—the synagogue, the Talmud Torah, our house—I could not find a trace. It's just a little island, but if you ever went to live in another country and come back to the place where you were born, it's a feeling you cannot describe. Even though there's nothing there, nothing. Just a ground. Like people come back and they kiss the earth—this is the way you feel.

My husband went swimming like he used to do when he was a little boy. He used to swim like a fish—you know, dive under and come up way out. So he tried to do it again. I said, "He's going to be left in this Sea of Marmara." One day he went twice. He said, "I've got to do it one more time before we leave."

I had four babies over twenty years. I was healthy, worked hard—I've been working hard a long time. But I'm happy working hard, busy either knitting or baking or whatever. I can't see doing nothing when I can do one little inch of needlepoint. I want to make an afghan for every grandchild.

Family is so important and these years are so important, especially for the little grandchildren that come here and say, "Can I sleep with you?" I have one that sleeps with me so close, he almost pushes me out of the bed. But these are the things he will remember, just like I remember. These are the things that are worth it.

I have good memories. I tell my kids, "When I die, don't cry. I had a beautiful life."

Sol Esfeld

Poland

I was born in Poland in 1898. Of course, life in Poland in those days, even as it is today, was very austere. We lived in a city called Plock, across from Warsaw on the Vistula River. Our family of six lived in a one-room flat. We had to go downstairs to the city pump and haul water upstairs for bathing and drinking. On one end of our rather large room was a kind of big Dutch oven with a large platform that would heat up during the day when we were cooking or baking. At night we four kids, three sisters and myself, used to all pile up on it and sleep there.

There was a lot of anti-Semitism because Poland was under the domination of the Russians. Occasionally the Cossacks would come to the city on horseback, get drunk, and cause all kinds of disturbances. Particularly they'd single out the Jews.

My father was a tailor, and he had some relatives in Dallas, Texas, so when he had an opportunity to emigrate to America, he seized it. He went by himself because we did not have enough money for all of us to go at the same time. There he got placed as a tailor, and about a year and a half later, he had earned enough to send for us. In those days, as today, Poland wouldn't allow emigration. The only way you could get out of the country was to bribe your way out. We were transported in a hay wagon and smuggled across the border into Germany. There we took a ship at Bremerhaven and landed in Galveston, Texas, the nearest port to where my father was.

As we got off the boat to go down to the railroad station, one of my sisters spotted a shiny object on the sidewalk. She picked it up, not knowing what it was, but Mother recognized it as a twenty-dollar gold piece. In the old country, they always used to say, when you were going to America, you weren't going to America, you were going to the *goldeneh medina*, to the Golden Land. So when my sister found this gold piece, my mother said, "This really is the *goldeneh medina!*" With that, we went into a small department store and were able to get a lot of new things for the entire family. In those days, a fine shirt cost a dollar or less, a pair of stockings a nickel or a dime.

So that was our first introduction to America.

We eventually came to Seattle around 1909 where my father also had some friends. It was a pioneering city, a growing city. Consequently, there were more opportunities than in Dallas, a long-established city. At the time we moved to Seattle, there were wooden streets. When they decided to pave the streets, they tore up these wooden blocks and we used them for firewood for two or three winters, which helped a great deal.

I finished grade school, eighth grade, when I was about fifteen. After that I went to business college for about six months. There I learned to be a stenographer and elementary bookkeeper. Then I got a job in an insurance company where I worked for six years. After that, I established my own insurance business.

I've always had an interest in community activities. I like to be with people. For some reason or other, I've always also had a knack for raising funds. In 1962 we decided to build a new Jewish home for the aged. My mother at that time was in her late eighties and not in good health. We had to find a nursing home for her, so she became a resident in the old Jewish home which housed thirty people, built in 1914. When I saw the conditions that prevailed, I decided then and there we'd have to do something about it. Since I opened my mouth, I became the fund-raising chairman. We needed $750,000, a lot of money at the time. We finally wound up with about $1,300,000, enough money not only to build the building but to furnish it completely. Mother lived long enough to move into and enjoy it.

The new building provided for about seventy residents, double the old house. In 1973 we needed to double the capacity once again. We decided to build another building to connect with the present one, at a cost of about $1,750,000, more than had ever been raised in the Jewish community before. A few of us got together and said, "Nothing is impossible if you're determined to do it." We worked at it for four years, and wound up with $3,600,000. So now we have a home that houses 145 residents, all paid for, completely furnished.

I always believe in the democratic process of letting people speak and give their version of things, but after that is all done, you must put everything together and use your own best judgment. I was never deterred or intimidated because people would say, "Well, this isn't necessary, or this can't be done." If you followed all these doomsayers, you couldn't accomplish very much.

Mitzi Fink

Czechoslovakia

I remember it so well. I was twenty-nine in 1938 and had been married for two years. We heard the news at six in the morning that Hitler is coming to Czechoslovakia. It was a terrible day, dark and raining. As old as I get, I'll never forget the day they marched in. Everyone was beside themselves and tried to form with their families and friends to get out. But how to get out? We needed papers that were so difficult to get. Documents that really meant the difference between life and death. And so we tried very, very hard and my husband and I made the last train out of Czechoslovakia. Only a few hundred people were able to get out.

The train was full of immigrants. Going through Germany was rough with their border search, but we made it. We made it with ten marks and a suitcase. When one can only bring a suitcase and must pack in such a haphazard manner, one grabs the silliest things, things I'd never use, like linens. The valuable things I left.

All my Jewish friends who stayed in Czechoslovakia perished. My friends who had babies thought, "Where can we go with children?" And the older and handicapped people I knew . . . how could they run to another country?

I was hoping my parents would come after us. They were about fifty at the time. We thought, "Once we are out, we will try to help them and they will be just fine." When we got to England, we tried to send for them but they couldn't get out. And so my parents perished. One has guilt feelings . . . like leaving a sinking ship. I can still see them standing there. It seems such a terrible amount of people, six million.

But we never knew it could happen. Now we should know. And we should learn from that experience because it could happen again. One has to tell the next generation. I think the young people don't know enough. It has been a long time, almost forty years. What I would tell people is to value freedom, to speak out and not go along if things are not right.

John Frankel

Denmark

We were four boys in my family. When I was six, we moved from Copenhagen to Germany. Two of us were born in Denmark and two of us were born in Germany. We were Orthodox people and my father wanted to give us a Jewish education. It was not possible in Denmark at that time. Hamburg was the city that had the Jewish school. I finished high school in Germany and then decided not to go to the University, but to go into business instead.

In 1923 we had an inflation in Germany. We got paid at noontime because at noontime the new exchange rates came out. The money was sometimes devalued within an hour or so. One time, I got paid and by the time I walked around the corner, I could just buy one bar of chocolate with my whole wages from the week. In 1929 I lost my job. I had a good friend who was a supervisor on a passenger boat to America. I thought, "Instead of drawing unemployment, I'll take the chance and get hired on the boat." I worked as a supervisor in the Jewish kitchen. I made several trips to America, but my impression of America at that time was not so good. I thought, "If ever I had to move to America, I would not stay in New York."

From Hitler we didn't know much at that time, but he was already working in the underground to take the government over. I made several trips to America, but then landed a job in Germany with a lawyer as a clerk. I was there three years, and then, suddenly one morning, the Gestapo came and arrested my boss, his father and his brother. And I alone was left. They didn't take me. The next day, I returned to Denmark. I had some connections and got permission to work there for two years, from 1933 to 1935. I learned leather cutting for shoes. When the two years were up, they wouldn't let me stay anymore and I had nowhere to go. It was very difficult for immigrants, so I went back to Germany. It was wrong to do, but I had personal reasons. My mother and brothers and future wife were still there. I found a very good position with the Jewish administration in Hamburg. In 1937 I married my wife and we lived in the house belonging to the mother of my wife.

Then came the infamous Crystal Night, November 10, 1938. All the beautiful synagogues in our city were destroyed by fire. They burned them down . . . like nothing. That night they arrested, in Germany alone, eighty thousand Jews and put them in concentration camps. I was in there too. I was five and a half weeks in there until they let us out again with the agreement we would pay money or be arrested again. It was five and a half weeks too long. I have seen enough. I have not talked much about it, but as the time goes by, it reflects always upon your future life. When I got out, I was very sick. We decided to try for America.

But it took us three years to fight with the American government to let us come. The situation got worse and worse while we were there. The Jews were put under curfew. We couldn't buy in any regular stores, we couldn't use public transportation, we couldn't travel. They finally gave us a visa in 1941. The transportation was arranged by the Jewish Administration. We paid our own transportation with what little money we had left that the government did not take away. We had only two suitcases and three dollars left to take with us. We went by train from Hamburg to Berlin. And in Berlin, we entered a train which was sealed off and darkened. We were transported by way of South Germany, France, and then to the Spanish border. On the border between France and Spain, we saw the last Germans. Half of the train station was French and half was Spanish. After we moved over to the Spanish side, they couldn't do anything to us any more. We came over to America on a freighter which carried fourteen hundred Jews. We paid for first-class transportation and we got a place in the hold of the boat where they put rows of bunks, for the people to live.

The boat landed in New York finally, in August 1941. Once we arrived in America, we wanted to live somewhere that was the best place for a Jewish life. I thought of Seattle as we already had some people here from Hamburg. I was one hour in Seattle and I had a job in the luggage business. Soon after, I found a job with the railroads and stayed with it for twenty-eight years. I was not lazy. My wife worked also many years. When I stopped working, my wife was a few years younger, but I told her to stop too. We are enjoying retirement together. I have a hobby collecting stamps and spend many hours in the library. When you have seen lots of things and you've seen so many sad things in your life, you are thankful for everything that is good.

Newman Glass

Rumania

If I stop to remember, if I stop to think . . . all the things I've done in my life and the places I've been, one thing runs into the other and there is so much to say I could spend days and days. I don't know where to begin. You could read my poetry. That would tell you all you want to know. Or I could paint a picture of the little town where I was born and lived until I was twenty years old.

Buhush was a little town in Moldova, Rumania. It had about five hundred families and seventy or eighty percent of them were Jewish. The town center consisted of three streets. All around in the country-side was mountains. There were no lights in Buhush. They had lamp posts that burned kerosene. An old man went around every evening to light the lamps, and every morning he blew them out. That was his job. And there were no sewers. Alongside the street, in front of all the houses, was a trench where the water would drain from the mountains until it reached a lake outside of town. As a result, every house had a little bridge from the porch to the street. The streets were never paved, just dirt, and when the rain came, there was mud up to your ankles. When the rain stopped, there was sunshine and all the mud would dry up and become yellow powder. The horse carts drove by and raised clouds of dust so you couldn't see for ten minutes. Women got up in the morning and poured buckets of water on the street to settle the dust and freshen the air.

There were nine children in my family. My mother was frail and beautiful. My father took care of her just like a little baby. He wouldn't let her bend down to tie her shoelaces. We weren't rich. My father had a hard time making a living to feed that many mouths. He did different things, but one of his jobs was to be secretary to the Rabbi.

This Rabbi was a holy man from generations of holy men. He was equal to the Pope. He was a *tzaddik*, a wise man. People would come from all over, even America, for consultations or blessings. My father worked in the foyer. He would greet the people, write down their names, where they came from, and what their desire was. Then he would take the information in to the Rabbi who would think what to do.

The Rabbi was rich. He wouldn't take money from the people; it wasn't dignified. But they would leave money, jewels, and gold on the table. He lived with his whole family in a big castle with two or three acres of land. His wife wore a diamond tiara and had jewels that would take your eyes out. People stood in line just to see them.

The big excitement in Buhush was Sunday, market day. The peasants came to town and drove in their horses, cattle, pigs, chickens, geese, and sheep to sell or trade. There were guys from Russia who wore long straps and ropes all along their bodies, and they had clothespins. Their job was to castrate the stallions. They hired us kids for ten or fifteen cents to hold the horses down and operated right there on the ground. What a sight! We called the men Cossacks because they were so brutal.

During the week, it was compulsory for kids to go to school. We went to a government school and the Jewish community was allowed to have their own teachers. We had a *melamed* who taught the Prophets, the Kings, and the Torah. A lot of the gentile kids were anti-Semitic. They would pick on the younger Jewish kids, ambush them, beat them up, cut off their buttons and empty their pockets. I was at that time about fifteen, sixteen years old. About ten of us organized ourselves to fight the anti-Semites. We even had the approval of the Rabbis to take care of them. And we did. We took care of them all right.

In the evening, boys and girls would come together in the square. A store there, run by a Bulgarian, sold ice cream, sodas, and peanuts with the shells. We would treat the girls to a drink and walk in the square. The street that led to the train station had a lot of tall grass and weeds on the side. We walked down there with the girls, sat in the tall grass, and made love. People drove by from out of town and saw the youngsters alongside the road there, making love.

It was a romantic town.

I don't know where to stop. There is so much to tell, so many anecdotes about the *shtetl* . . . about my life. In my younger days I was so humble. I didn't like to talk about myself or to show off. Now, it's too late.

Marion Glazer

Poland

I don't know what Warsaw looks like now because I haven't been back. I'm not even interested in going back, but when I lived there it was one of the most beautiful cities in the world. Every street had an oval grass area with flowers and trees. We lived in an apartment with a court that was enclosed with an iron fence. My grandparents on my father's side were farmers, and I remember riding out to the farm. That was a happy occasion. There were beautiful poppies, all different colors everywhere. All the people had poppies growing.

Poland was under the czar's control, so the Cossacks and the pogroms were right there. The Cossacks would just as soon kill you as look at you. There wasn't a working man who didn't leave home without a knife for protection. You were afraid to say you were Jewish. You were Polish and that's it. One night, there was a pounding on our door. The Cossacks wanted to come in. We kids had papers with our ABC's on it and the men looked for propaganda on the pages to see if my mother was against the government. If they had found anything, she would have immediately been taken out and shot. They don't monkey around.

My father was here in the United States four years before he saved enough to send for my mother and five children. There was a little one he never even saw until we came to the United States. He fixed my mother up in Europe and left.

We traveled by ship and railroad. We didn't know anything about planes then, seventy years ago. My mother was very beautiful and one of the sailors on the ship fell in love with her. He was seasick and my mother was nursing him. So we were not third class or steerage. We were second class. We got oranges, hard-boiled eggs, the royal treatment. The sailor sneaked everything to us. There were two English words I learned on the ship, "All right" and "Come on," because that's all anybody said to us.

When we got to Castle Garden, a person had to be healthy and have at least thirty dollars on them before they could get into the United States. My mother didn't have the money so they wouldn't let us in. We had to stay there five days until my father sent the money to us. We slept on benches in the waiting room.

When we got to Seattle, I was put in the first grade. In six years I made my eight grades and in six months I had not one bit of an accent. My name in Polish is Manya. My Yiddish name is Miriam. So my teacher says, "We'll call you Marion." I thought Marion was a beautiful name. It sounded so American. I had a lot of fun when I was a kid. I was always in trouble, a real tomboy. I used to go to the lake and get on the twenty-five foot dive and down I would go. I wasn't afraid of anything. There was nobody who could beat me swimming. One time, I was on a big ferry and the kids dared me to dive off the top of the ferry and swim back to the picnic grounds. So I did it. I certainly did. When I became engaged to my husband, my father said to him, "I give you six months with that woman." We were married fifty-eight and a half years.

My husband is gone now but I'm still involved. I'm the main soprano in the choir at the Golden Age Club and have been in nine plays. I haven't changed that much since I was a kid. We had a bazaar at the Golden Age Club and I was chairman of the pastries. I got up in front of the people about a month before the bazaar and said, "Folks, listen. If I don't get enough pastry, I'm going to be a very unhappy person." And in your life, you never saw as much pastry as we had at the bazaar. Beautiful cakes, and people who couldn't bake brought money. I'm not bragging, but when I get up in front of the people, they listen.

Ida Goldfine

Russia

I walk five miles every morning, and I think this is what keeps me going. When I walk, I always have a smile on my face, and the people I pass become my friends. If you are understanding and tolerant with people, you will have a lot of friends. To me, this is the fulfillment of life.

My mother had twelve children and she never was to a doctor. When she passed away, she just fell asleep. She was close to my age when she passed away, eighty-seven. I don't mind telling you my age because age is only numbers. What difference does that make? It depends on the person, how they keep themselves and what they are involved with, if they keep their minds occupied all the time and don't sit and wait to die. I have always kept occupied.

In Europe when I was a child I had an older brother. In 1905 there was a brewing like the revolution, so the Cossacks picked up every young man and put him in jail. They ran around on their horses and picked up everyone who was walking; and if they knew the house they came from, they'd go to their home and look for socialistic literature. They came to our house and never found anything, but they picked up my brother anyway and put him in jail.

My parents didn't know what to do. My mother would bake bread so I should take it to jail to my brother. I was about nine years old—just the age where I could carry a basket and take the food to him. So one time I came to him and he said, "You know, they're going to send us all to Siberia. When you go home, you tell Daddy and Mother and see what they can do to help me out."

So I went home and told them, and what could they do? They started to cry. Siberia was the end of the world. I decided to go to the supposedly governor. I don't know who he was but he was a Russian official of some sort and I came crying. I didn't have shoes on because we only wore them in the winter and this happened in the fall.

The people wouldn't let me in. The two policemen who were sitting in the front office said, "Tell me what you want."

I said, "I can't tell you. I want to see the head of this office."

So they look at me, they see a little urchin, and they either felt sorry for me or I looked peculiar—I don't know—but they went to the official and he said, "Send her in."

I came in there and I fell on my knees. I felt so terrible. I cried and cried. He said, "Stop crying and tell me what you want."

So I did. I said, "My brother is in jail. But my brother is not a Socialist."

He said, "How can you prove it?"

I said, "I can tell you this. If you let my brother out, I promise you, I'll take him to America and he won't be in your way."

The official said, "How can you go to America? You don't have any money."

I said, "I have a brother in America and I'll write to him and he'll send us tickets."

They let my brother go, and this is what brought me to America. You need *chutzpah* and that's what I have.

Daniel Haguel

Greece

Thessalonika is the place Alexander the Great was born. It is one of the most beautiful places in the world, all surrounded with water. Its borders are with Albania, Yugoslavia, Bulgaria, and Turkey. There were many Jewish people there at one time. Originally we came from Spain when Queen Isabella threw us out. Before World War I, three-quarters of the population of Thessalonika was Jewish. But when I was a kid, there was some sort of anti-Semitism and the Jewish saw trouble ahead. Little by little they emigrated. You know how it is in every country. Something goes wrong and they blame the Jewish. Most of the time we got along pretty good in Greece. The Jews don't bother nobody. Sometimes we turn the other cheek, sometimes we fight. It was that way all our lives, for two thousand years.

In 1942 when the Germans came, our town was sixty thousand Jews. In 1945 after our liberation, there were nineteen hundred of us left. The Germans came and in six months destroyed seven or eight hundred years of Jewish life. They burned and destroyed our cemeteries, synagogues, businesses. Nothing was left. Nothing. They destroyed everything. After they finished with the things, they started on the people. They took us to Poland in wagons, to Auschwitz and Birkenau.

In Birkenau there was a big sign, *Arbeit Macht Frei*, the work gives freedom. I worked in the coal mines, fifteen hundred meters down with no food, no water. They chained us two-and-two. Everyone of us had broken ankles because the chains were so short we would hit with our feet the person in front of us. If we didn't hurry, they shot us.

My shift was from four o'clock in the afternoon to two o'clock in the morning. They didn't give you time to think. They didn't leave you for one minute alone. They always wanted to occupy your mind because they knew in five seconds a Jew could build a building with an idea.

We were so confused, not one person murdered but millions of us. I used to say my Shema. I would say, "Shema Yisrael, not me God." We would pray, "Please God, not now. Today I want to survive." Today become important. We had to have something to hold onto. But sometimes, in despair, I would curse my God.

In January 1945 the Russians were coming. They were so close we could hear the cannons. The Nazis wanted to finish killing the Jews but they had no time. So they took us at night, walking. There were fifteen thousand of us. We walked in rows of five. On the outside were the Germans and tanks, on the inside the Jews. Twenty-two hours a day walking, without food, without water. Every three or four days they would give us a piece of bread. Nothing else. If you walked slow, they shot you. We had two hours off. Everyone who tried to sit, they couldn't get up. We walked January, February, March, and April. We walked from Poland to Germany, from the Russian front to the American front. I walked with my friend Morris. I said, "Morris, don't stop. If you sit, you're gonna die. Let's go. We can hear the cannons. Please don't die." We survived because we didn't sit.

On the twenty-third of April we see something different. Before, every day the people got killed and they let them lie there on the road. That day we saw horse-carts behind us and they were putting bodies on the carts. We wondered why. At nine o'clock in the morning, an American airplane with four cylinders flew so low you could see the pilots with the machine guns. There were about five hundred of us left and we continued to walk, five in a row with the Germans on both sides of us. The bullets started to go. They hit to our right, they hit to our left; not one bullet hit in the middle. The SS started to fall or run into the forest. We can't run. Something is happening. Then we see over one hundred American tanks in a horse-shoe turn around and surround us. We hear over a loudspeaker, "Everybody in the forest, come out with your hands up."

That was my liberation.

Goldie Handlin

Russia

I can't remember too much of Odessa because I was six years old when we came here, but I do remember the beautiful park. My mother would take me there every Saturday. And that park was right near the Black Sea. My mother would hold me by the hand and we would go down the wide steps to the sea. I was an only child and she would sit on a bench and watch me while I played.

We lived in a brick apartment building with a wooden gate that locked and a courtyard. It was quite modern with faucets for hot and cold. The washroom was in one part of the building. I had a bad experience in that washroom.

In Odessa they had a lot of pogroms on the Jews. I was playing in the courtyard and all of a sudden, somebody yells, "They are coming for us!" My mother opened the window and hollered, "All you children, run to the washroom." And of course, when I heard my mother's voice, I ran. The parents locked us in. As youngsters we got scared and started crying. But the older kids, they were smart. They told us to keep quiet and not make a sound. But we could hear men yelling, "Where are the Jews? Where are the Jews?" I didn't know what it meant, but I knew I was a Jew. When it was over, a couple mothers came down and let us out. They said, "Now you're all right." We were quiet and that's what saved us. When you're a kid in that kind of situation, you learn to be smart.

My father died when I was very young. I had an uncle in America who sent my mother tickets to go to him. My mother, with all the hardships she had, still didn't want to leave. The tickets were good for a year and she wore them around her neck in a little pouch. I cried and cried because I wanted to go to America. Finally the last two weeks of her tickets, she said, "I guess we'll go." And she started packing.

That was 1906. We went on the boat and came to New York first. Then we took the train to be with my aunt and uncle in Iowa. On the train, we were sitting across from a couple. The man took out some fruit. I happened to glance over and saw a banana. I had never seen one before and I thought, "What in the world is that?" The man saw me glancing at it so he gave it to me. I couldn't figure out how to eat it. My mother saw it and she grabbed it out of my hand and said, "You mustn't touch it. We don't know what it is." She opened the window and threw it out.

When I was eighteen in Iowa, I had a wonderful job in a department store and I went to school and took up bookkeeping. I was very efficient in those days. I had a vacation coming up so my cousin and I took the train to Seattle to visit another aunt. On the Fourth of July the Jewish people had a picnic and I met my husband, Dave. From that day on, he came to see me at my aunt's every day. When I saw the lakes and mountains, I fell in love with Seattle and decided to stay. I found a job and was so thrilled about it. I got engaged to Dave after six weeks, and three months later we got married.

Then all of a sudden, he tells me I can't work any more. Women didn't work in those days unless they were single. If they were married, their husbands provided for them. It was like a law. I said, "Please let me work. I have a wonderful job and I just got it."

He said, "No. I have three sisters and if you worked I'd be ashamed to face them."

It wasn't like now. I cheered for Women's Liberation because why shouldn't we have the same privileges as the men? So I was active instead. I had three children and was President of two PTA's at the same time. I never was depressed.

Take everything as it comes good or bad and don't worry. My mother said a good lesson: "Life is like a wave in the ocean—it goes up and down, up and down."

Arthur Lagawier

Holland

From my youth in Amsterdam, I was imbued with a love for Judaism. When I was three years old, my mother's father started to teach me Hebrew and the Bible. He did it in such a wonderful way that I never got tired of listening to him, and when after two or three hours, my mother came and said, "Papa, what do you want? This is a little child, let him play," I didn't want to leave because the way he was teaching was so fascinating that I couldn't imagine doing anything more pleasant.

He began teaching me Hebrew with the letter *B*, the first letter of the Bible. The name of this letter in Hebrew is *bayt*, and *bayt* means also "a house." He said, "A house must be open like this letter, so that when a person comes to you, he doesn't have to stand outside and wait." He told me a story which the Talmud tells about Abraham. He said, "Abraham was our great, great grandfather, and he had a house which had four doors from four sides. From wherever somebody came, always a door, and the doors were always open." In this way, he taught me all the letters, and the principles of Judaism, and the principles of Ethics. The younger a child is, the easier it is to teach him.

He kept it up. And then he died. I was born in 1901. He died in 1907. I was six years old and we had finished the five books of Moses. My grandfather made in me a love for learning. It wasn't inborn, but it is true that in our family, I have a list of the roots that goes back to the 1400s, and the men were all Rabbis, uninterrupted. So I thought, I don't want to interrupt it, so I will also study to become a Rabbi.

But . . . I needed a teacher. Now the one grandfather had died. My Grandfather Lagawier was the most learned Talmudic scholar in the city. He was an encyclopaedia in Judaism. So I asked, "Grandpa, will you study with me Talmud?" He said, "I will only study with you Talmud if you have a good complete knowledge of the twenty-four books of the Bible. You have only studied five books of Moses. There are still eight books of the Prophets and eleven books of the Scriptures. When you have a good knowledge of all of them, then we can study the Talmud because the Talmud is really a commentary of the Biblical texts, and it is no use to study discussions of texts with which you are not one hundred percent familiar."

So I started to study for myself the other books. The librarian of the big Judaica and Hebraica library in Amsterdam, a second cousin, gave me the books I needed in grammar, in philosophy, in theology. I didn't have to go very much to school, so I spent all the time in study.

My father had a big diamond-cutting plant. He didn't want me to become a Rabbi or a Ph.D. He said, "Study as much as you want, but I don't want you to have that title." My father said, "I only have one child. I'm getting old, I have a big business. If you have a good business and the right people to work for you, you can go home at five o'clock and study." So I learned all the work that goes with diamonds. When Hitler came, he took away what we had.

We escaped with very little. My daughter was eight when we came to Miami through Cuba in 1942, and then we were half a year in New York. I asked a man where the farthest place was from New York, and he told me Seattle. We came here, and I had a diamond business again. I did very well, but when I was sixty-five years old, I gave up my business and I said if I have still several years to live, I'm going to use them to spread a little more knowledge and a little more understanding of Judaism because I feel that Judaism is a recipe for a better world.

I taught the children what I believe about Judaism, about God as a plan, an idea, a program how to live. I should have been stronger. Only a few—five, six, from all the hundreds of students I taught as a volunteer—learned what I was trying to teach.

One day one of the Rabbis here met me in the street downtown. He said, "Arthur, I know you're doing a nice job with children. You're teaching them Hebrew and the Hebrew religion. Very nice. But somebody told me you told them you don't believe in the miracle of Chanukah." I said, "What miracle do you mean? There are several miracles." He said, "You told them in a class, 'If ever somebody tells you that there was only enough oil left for one night, don't believe it because this is nonsense. If it burned eight nights, then there was enough for eight nights.'" I said, "Yes, I said that. But I also said there is a much greater miracle. I celebrate Chanukah because Chanukah was a victory over powers which were evil. It was not a war for territory. It was a war in which people stood up and sacrificed for their ideals, for their religion and their langauge. And that light, that fire which burned in their hearts is still burning today, two thousand years later. That," I said, "is the miracle."

Ludwig Lobe

Germany

When I grew up, the German Jews believed they had reached the apex of Jewish life. Actually they had reached the high point of assimilation into Western European culture. Since Napoleon's time, many German Jews did not live in ghettos. Even before his time, when they were living in ghettos, they still spoke German. When I came to America, I was surprised to hear Jewish people speaking Yiddish, which I had not heard and could not understand.

Yet you can't escape your identity in a country where everybody's religion is on high school diplomas, birth certificates, and death certificates. In the Rhineland, after graduating from the *Gymnasium*, I studied law. After law school, I worked as an intern in a prosecuting attorney's office. Hitler came in January 1933. In September 1933 I got my letter.

I had a passport which allowed me to go back and forth from Germany. It's awfully nice to have someone whom you helped pass an exam in high school. Even if he's a Nazi, he becomes very grateful.

I eventually went to Geneva after traveling around Europe, looking for a place to settle. There I did postgraduate work in law and met my future wife. In 1936 she and I decided to get married and to leave Europe. We got married twice, in England first at a civil registry, and three days later in Germany by a Rabbi with our families. After our honeymoon, we returned to Geneva to pick up some things. We passed by the American Consulate where we had tried several times before to get a visa. My wife said, "Well, let's go back in again and see what happens." There was a new consul. He asked her how she got her English accent. She told him she had lived in England and we had been married in Hampstead just a few weeks earlier. The consul said he had also been married in Hampstead just a few weeks earlier. The next day we got our visa.

Within the month, we came to New York. I started out as a floorwalker in a five-and-ten-cent store. I got $2.00 a day, and lasted two days. I then worked as a bookkeeper for five months, after which we decided to seek our fortune away from New York. We bought a small car and started out with a bunch of papers, letters of introduction to every town in the United States. For about six weeks we traveled America. We ended up in Seattle, arriving in August 1937, where we both found jobs almost immediately. Between us, we earned $35.00 a week. We lived comfortably with car, apartment, lunches for 35 cents, and food for the week from the Public Market for $5.00.

One day an accountant who handled the books where I worked asked me about my education. He said, "You're a lawyer. Why don't you come to our office and start reading tax law and see what you can do?" I accepted his offer. My first paycheck working for him was $7.50 because I worked fifteen hours, 50 cents an hour. Eventually I worked as an accountant full time, took the necessary exams, and in good time became a full-fledged partner.

One thing leads to another. I have been involved in many civic activities—in aging, in health care, hundreds of things. Only in America is it possible for an ordinary citizen to participate in community affairs and decision-making. My specific interests in most cases center on the financial side of organizations, that they stay healthy, and on the human side, by staying healthy, that they can do the work they are supposed to do. I listen to people and make my decisions based on what I hear, not on what I think I should hear.

The first time we returned to Europe was 1960, taking our sons to see the places we had grown up and lived. The first time you return to the German border, you get a very fast heartbeat. Approaching from Holland, I recognized the roads where some of us, then German interns in the legal system, had helped people flee Nazi Germany.

In my home town, some people recognized me immediately, probably because one of my sons looked like me when I was young. One day we went into one of the old town restaurants where the old crowd used to have a few beers after a day's work. One of the elderly waiters with a white beard circled our table and said in German, "Don't I know you? As a matter of fact, didn't you used to sit in that corner over there with all the court attendants?"

I realize how lucky I have been to come to America with its freedoms. I always think about what would have happened to me if I would have stayed in Germany and they would not have been anti-Semitic. I would probably have been in the German Army and dead.

Lucie Loeb

Switzerland

We had a wonderful life in Switzerland. I was born in Zurich in 1895. I had one brother and three sisters. One sister had gone to the Conservatory of Music in Zurich. When she left for Lausanne (every girl had to go to a boarding school in Lausanne where they got their education and learned French), my mother went to her piano teacher and asked if she would take me in her place. The teacher said, "Oh, yes, any of your children I would take." So I had a fine teacher from the beginning—I was about nine years old—and that did it. I went with music to the very end when I got my diploma from the Conservatory of Music in Zurich. I still practice every day, at least an hour.

My husband and I knew each other for seven years before we got married because the First World War came in between. Every four months the men had to go into military service because they had to watch the borders. Switzerland was never involved in the war but it was very close, surrounded by war. For a while, we were very anxious because the Germans wanted to go through Switzerland. But they knew if they would come, Switzerland had all those hills and mountains, and the mountains were all mined. So they knew if they came and touched it, that would be their end. We were a small country, but we were prepared.

We left Switzerland for my children, a son and a daughter. Once, one of the teachers said to my boy, "You know, a boy like you shouldn't be in *Gymnasium*. You should go to a *Handelsschule*," to a commercial school. When he came home and told us, I said to my husband, "Now we'll go. With such anti-Semitism, I am not going to stay."

It took courage, all of a sudden, to pack up and go. We couldn't tell my family until the very last. The very last we told them we were going to emigrate. All the relatives thought it was terrible we were going to leave. We were unusual. There were very few Swiss emigrants.

We left in 1941. My brother had already come to Seattle. He had been told how beautiful it was, like Switzerland with the mountains. We stayed first in New York at a cousin's. She offered us her house because she had just moved with her new husband into an apartment. So we had that house and it was almost as if we were home because we had the pictures of my parents and relatives in the house. We never felt strange here for one moment.

After we moved to Seattle, I taught piano privately and did a lot of accompanying. I played for the dancers Gerald Arpino and Robert Joffrey. They got very famous, retired now. My brother had a Swiss pastry shop. When he had a bad day—they were not supposed to keep the pastries for the next day—he always gave them to me and said, "Bring it! Bring it to your dancers!" To this day when Arpino sees me, he always says, "Lucie, if it wouldn't have been for you, I would have starved to death." He told me, "See, always I would dance a little and then I would go back to your desk and get some pastry, and then dance some more."

My husband was happy here that he could mow the lawn on Sunday. For him, that was the most wonderful thing. In Switzerland on Sunday, you couldn't do anything.

So long I have been gone from Switzerland, over forty years. I have gone back only once, after the war. And then, you know, everything seemed so small and small minded. I thought, "I couldn't live here any more." I have a niece. I asked her once—I wanted to know something and she wouldn't give me the information—"Why are you so secretive?" And she said, "You know we are in a small country. If we are not secretive, we have no privacy." I never realized that when we were in Switzerland, but when we moved here, I understood what she said. In America you do what you want to. If you want to mow your lawn on Sunday, you mow your lawn on Sunday. And that's what my husband liked so much.

Walter Lowen

Germany

I left Germany on July 29, 1936. Why I know the date so well is because it was my birthday. I was born in Munich and lived in Munich for thirty-three years. My family goes back in southern Germany since 1740, which is quite a few years. I had there what they call a family tree. Our name was so good that when I left in 1936, Germany gave me a passport good to travel all over the world for five years.

Our family had a retail business in Germany in ladies' hats, millinery, for many, many years, which I eventually joined. I waited until my father passed on, and then I left. I could see the danger, being so close to Hitler and the Nazis in Munich. Many of my school friends, former school friends, were becoming big Nazis.

At first my family, generally, couldn't believe that I would leave everything and just go. Naturally I had to give everything I had, except my furniture, which they allowed me to take with me. But I was not afraid. I had a good education, and I still believe it's what you have in your head, it's what helps you wherever you go.

Before I left, one of the unforgettable evenings was the last concert Bruno Walter, at that time the head of the Munich Symphony, gave before he had to leave Germany. They played Beethoven's Ninth Symphony, and the good-bye applause lasted over an hour in an audience mostly of gentiles. He was one of the first ones who had to leave. There was nothing one could do.

I had an affidavit to come to Seattle from a man there who had relatives in Germany. At that time it was a long way from Munich to Seattle. I started working after four days here for the family who had sent me the affidavit. They owned the Alaska Fur Company. I did not know much about the fur business, but I learned pretty good. Then the war came, and we were engaged in making cold weather clothing for the military. I was frozen to my job.

I was intrigued with Alaska, especially the native business, and I started to build my own business up slowly after the war. I was not a youngster, but I traveled Alaska for thirty years, for selling purposes. It was pretty rough in those days up there, but I went because I felt there would be less discrimination than there would be any other place, which was true.

We've built a pretty good business. The first years were very rough because Alaska was very small. As Alaska was built up, our business was built up. I've sold more totem poles in my life than anyone else in the world.

I have the natives in every day, ten, twelve natives. They look to me as their father. I have learned to talk to them. As much as I can help them, I'll try to help them.

There's quite an interest in Indians in Germany today. Three months ago I had a visit from three colonels from the German Luftwaffe who were in Seattle to pick up three AWACS planes from Boeing. I was a little surprised to see three German military men with lots of stars walking in my place. It took me a little while to really believe what they wanted—to buy some totem poles. They were surprised to find someone who spoke the Bavarian dialect selling totem poles. They were also surprised that I would still know every street in Munich and could tell them things they didn't know because they were too young at the time.

We were extremely fortunate that none of our family had to go to jail or the concentration camps. In 1938 my mother left Germany for this country just on the last boat before the war started. My three sisters and their families all came here before her. All my family came to this country.

I married two years after I came here, a girl from Seattle. We had two children, a boy and a girl. Both of my children became my partners in my business and are taking over, but I am still quite active. And now I am being paged. See, somebody has problems in Alaska. And now, see, my carvers are here waiting for me.

Sam Bension Maimon

Turkey

I was born in 1908 in Brusa, in Asia Minor, about sixty miles from Istanbul. My father later assumed a position as Rabbi in Rodosto, so we lived there about ten years before we came here in 1924. One of the two Sephardic synagogues in Seattle was made up of about sixty to eighty members that came from that same town. Because they liked my father so much, they brought us all over, eight children and my parents.

We had a very rough ocean voyage. My mother got very sick, so as soon as we got in New York, she had to be hospitalized. We landed at Ellis Island and stayed there six or seven days. One night after supper, they showed us a movie, an old Charlie Chaplin movie, I still remember. When the movie was over, one of the guards is calling, "Englishmen! Englishmen! Come this way!" And from another door, a guard was calling, "Frenchmen! Frenchmen! Come this way!" And we, all the rest, were put in a mess hall with bunks.

So I said to myself, "I'm going with the Englishmen and see what happens." Instead of bunks, they give us beautiful private rooms. I spent the night in a beautiful room. Meantime, my dad and my brothers were looking for me all over. In the morning as soon as they saw me, they said, "Where have you been? We've been looking for you, going crazy!" So I told them all about it. That day my dad inquired about all this discrimination through an interpreter that knew English and Spanish. That man explained to the authorities that I had gone with the Englishmen the night before. From that night on, they gave us a private room.

My mother got well and we were put on the train the night after Rosh Hashanah. When we got to Chicago, we had to stay almost a whole day. Mother saw at the depot hot running water and registers for heat. In Turkey, we never heard of hot running water. So she made a laundry. We were there about seven hours, and she used those seven hours to make a laundry. She had clothes hanging all over the registers.

In 1959 when we made a trip to New York and we stopped in Chicago, I said to my wife, "Come with me and I'll show you where my mother hanged the laundry," and the place was still there!

When we came to Seattle in 1924, I did not know a word of English. Everybody that came from out of the country went to special classes for foreigners at a school with teachers who knew how to project and teach the English language. The first day of school, they asked me my name. I said, "My name is Bension Shalom Maimon." They said, "That's too long. Why don't you make it Americanized? Short!" So I asked my friends what others did who had the name "Bension Shalom." They said they shortened it to Sam. So that's how I am Sam.

I was sixteen already when we came, and made up my mind I had to go to high school, so I used to read and use two or three dictionaries. The principal saw that I was very earnest in learning English, so he made it possible for me to go to summer school. The next September, they enrolled me in high school.

I finally needed two credits to graduate, but when the Depression came, my dad needed some help, and I had a job I didn't want to give up. In 1932 we opened our own grocery store where we handled everything that the Sephardim used to like. Everything imported, like olives, salt fish, olive oil, different types of pasta. We even handled vegetables not handled by other stores, because in those days the people used to cook the way they cooked in Turkey. We stayed in that store until 1969 when we were forced to leave because of riots in that part of the city.

Even when I was in business, at night as soon as I'd have supper, I'd go to my room and read. I knew Hebrew, but I educated myself in Hebrew, Rabbinics, and the Mishnah. I've had this love of literature and culture for a long time, even when I was in business. When I got out of business and got involved in teaching—at the Hebrew Academy and at the university—I had more time to study a lot of books and articles that explain a lot of practices in the Sephardic culture. Our synagogue publishes a little pamphlet once a month. Every month for the last ten or twelve years, I write an article in it, all on things of Sephardic and Ladino interest.

In 1977 they gave me a testimonial dinner for forty years' service to the synagogue. They sure surprised me at that dinner. One of the chairmen's wives was a bookkeeper for the principal at the high school I had attended over fifty years before. As soon as they heard through her that I needed two credits to graduate, they maneuvered it and talked to the school board and the principal. At that dinner, they gave me a cap and robe, an Honor Society pin, and a diploma. So I got my diploma finally.

It's no crime to boast, is it?

Sarah Miller

Russia

I am one hundred years old. I come from a small town in Russia. Oh God, so many years ago. My father had a store with dry goods. I used to work in the store measuring by yards. Our family had enough to eat. We used to bake bread and cook dinners, but not everybody had enough to eat. It was a rotten life for the Jews. The Russian soldiers were terrible. They used sticks, they stole, they used to throw away anything they found in our rooms. They were common people. That's the trouble. They had no education and didn't know any better. They could do anything and they done it.

I got married when I was twenty-two or twenty-three. Everything was so different then, the way we lived. The matchmaker brought him to my house, he looked at me, he sees I'm all right, so we get married.

My parents gave us six hundred Russian dollars for a dowry and in a few years we used it to come to America. We had one baby already and I was pregnant on the boat. When we got to New York, I felt free. My baby was born and we stayed about a week. Then we went to Superior, Wisconsin. We had a nice life in Wisconsin. My husband had a business there, but he got sick and died. He worked too hard and so he is gone. Then I came to Seattle with my children. My uncle sent for us.

I used to go for walks and do the sewing and the knitting. I used to do lots of work with the hands. But not now, my eyes aren't so good. My cane is my friend. Sometimes, if you want to die, you can't. But I have a good daughter. You can give a medal to her. She takes care of me to live.

Eric Offenbacher

Germany

Most of my life, my profession was dentistry. I practiced dentistry in New York for forty-two years, the last years together with my wife who assisted me in the office. We decided to retire while we were in good health and able to make the choice ourselves. You begin to appreciate, when you are getting old and time is running out, how you cherish each hour, so you make them all count.

I am an amateur musicologist. Whatever I know about musicology, I taught myself with books and experience. Mozart is my special interest, my idol if you will. He appeals to me because he is so human—in his virtues, in his weaknesses. He excels in every field of music, and his operas especially show a remarkable insight into human beings. He loved life from any angle, and my own life would not be what it is today if it had not been for Mozart. That sounds silly, but it's true.

I had accumulated over the years a collection of 78 RPM recordings, some of which go back to 1900, comprising Mozart's vocal music. The University of Washington has been very happy to accept both this collection and my conditions that went with it—to transfer all these recordings onto tape so that the originals can be preserved and the tapes used by students for study.

I also have offered my services in National Public Radio broadcasts in which I have conducted classical music programs on a regular basis. These broadcasts give me a lot of pleasure, especially in the opportunity they provide to use some of my rare recordings.

I was born in Frankfurt am Main where for generations my mother's family lived. I was brought up in an Orthodox Jewish home and educated in an Orthodox day school. After graduation from high school, I was able in 1930, still before Hitler came to power, to start my dental studies at the University of Frankfurt. In 1934 I completed them and passed my exams without trouble, even though the professors appeared for the exams in brown shirts with swastika armbands and said, "Heil, Hitler!" and we Jews said, "Good morning." Nothing happened, but my diploma has a swastika on it which I have had to show all my life whenever I needed to present my credentials.

Soon after graduation, one of my professors came to me and said, "I can see you have no future in this country. It's better to leave while you can." He put me in touch with a friend of his, a professor in Phila-delphia, a German, with whom I eventually came to study.

I had an uncle in the United States, here since 1903, who sent me an affidavit. In September 1934 I left Germany. My parents had left at the beginning of 1934 because my father had seen this thing coming in his travels around Europe. He established a branch of his business in Amsterdam, and had to pay a small "flight tax" because he was fleeing the country. His fellow Jews told him he was crazy throwing money into the pockets of the Nazis, thinking this thing would blow over. My father, like a prophet, said, "The time will come probably when you will be glad if you can get out at all." And he was absolutely right. I was able to bring my parents over just before the Nazis moved into Holland in 1940.

After a year in Philadelphia in which I learned to speak English and to practice the American way of dentistry, I returned to New York where I had to pass my state boards. In the fall of 1936 I opened my office in Manhattan. When the war started, I volunteered twice to serve in the army, and was twice rejected for some very silly physical reasons. I didn't have to volunteer, but I felt I owed it to this country that had not only saved my life but given me an opportunity to start a new life and a new profession.

Suddenly, in the summer of 1943, the army contacted me again. They had, they said, "lowered the physical standards." I didn't hesitate. I got my orders to report to Dallas, Texas. Eventually, a colonel, known to be anti-Semitic, put me in an outfit that was ready to go overseas. I was supposed to go with a medical clearing company, the one way up on the front, picking up casualties that had been shot down and bringing them to the first-aid stations and the field hospitals.

I am a firm believer that God not only created the world but keeps on guiding the world in all its happenings, and especially the lives of individuals. My life is founded on this deep faith, and rooted still in Orthodox Jewish tradition. As always in my life, I feel the hand of God that helped me. Like a miracle, the night before we were to ship out, I was withdrawn from the outfit. The Table of Organization and Equipment had called for two captains to go with the soldiers. I was just a first lieutenant. The night before I was to go, a captain was ordered to replace me, and I stayed behind.

Albert Ovadia

Isle of Marmara

I was born in Turkey in 1888 on a small island across the water from Istanbul. It was rugged country, a lot of grape vineyards. Six months winter, six months summer. I got no brothers or sisters. I'm the only one. My father was a winemaker. I went to religious school and then when I was twelve years old I started to make a living. I worked for two years for free to learn the grocery trade. Then I worked for five dollars a year. It went up.

With that money I came to this country. I was eighteen years old when I first came here. My father was already here and my mother stayed in the old country. When I came to Seattle, I was a shoeshine boy. If you can't speak the language, it's all you can do. Sit down and make a shine. I saved a thousand dollars in four years.

My father went back to the old country, but before he left he told me I should get married. My future wife was in the old country at that time. I knew her since I was fourteen or fifteen and she was twelve. We were neighbors. So, after four years I went back. I stayed in Turkey six months and saw her every day. Finally, I wanted to come back to this country because what could I do there? I took the suitcase and went down to the dock to wait for the boat. I waited and waited. It didn't come that day. So I went back to my girlfriend and said, "Do you want to come to America? How about we get married and you come to America with me?" We came back here and I got a house for us for ten dollars a month. I sold fish for a living. We got along because things were cheap. Later on, I bought my own fish business. It was hard work, especially in the wintertime. My hands would freeze. I was there fifty years.

When I wasn't working, I was always interested in birds. I used to raise chickens, pigeons, ducks, and geese. I even raised eagles. In the old country, one of the shepherds brought a little eagle to the store where I was working. It got so big, it followed me around like a dog. You can't find them anymore because people killed them. I wouldn't kill a bird or anything. I wouldn't even kill a fly. If I find one in my room I catch it, open the window and let it out.

Now I am ninety-three years old. Only two of my six children are still alive. It makes you older when your children die. If it wasn't for that terrible thing of my children dying . . . it makes you very old.

Rachel Peha

Isle of Rhodes

The Isle of Rhodes was not so big, but always the people were together. Rich people, poor people, together and happy with what they had. Families were sweet with each other. Husbands and wives didn't have no arguments, only happy conversations.

Friday was cooking day and baking day. All the Jewish people knew—today is Shabbat. On Friday afternoon around two thirty, my mother would finish all the cooking. Around four o'clock, a special man would go around and call to the whole Jewish court, "It's time to light the candle." My mother would say to me, "Come on Rachel, it's time. Shabbat is coming." I was so excited. It was just like the bride is coming. At night at home, my father, my mother, and all the children around the table. My father used to say the prayers, and we were quiet to listen. It was peace.

I was a school child when we came to New York in 1916, fourteen years old. My whole family was there together except my oldest sister. She was married and living in Seattle. One day in New York, my mother said to my other sister and me, "We are all the family at the same table, eating, talking, laughing. I feel so sorry for your sister in Seattle. Send some pictures to her." So we sent our pictures.

My sister was so happy to get the pictures, she showed them to everybody. Two boys saw the pictures. One wants me and one wants my other sister. So my sister in Seattle wrote a nice letter to my mother: "Dear Mom, I give you news. Two nice boys. They want your daughters." My poor mother. Two daughters at the same time to get married. She said, "We'll see for Rachel later. She is too young. First I want her sister married." But the boy sent me his picture anyway, a beautiful looking boy, and my mother says, a nice boy. Then he sent me a letter and a hundred dollars for a ring. I got the ring right away. I never had a diamond before.

We came to Seattle in 1917. It was more like the Isle of Rhodes. My sister was engaged to the boy who wanted her from the picture. We were busy sewing by hand everything for the trousseau. The boy who wanted me from the picture would come every day and give me something. One day a beautiful corsage of gardenias, the next day a big cake, the next day ice cream, another day candy. I said, "Listen, every time you come here, you have to give me something? I don't want it." He said, "Money?" I said, "No, please, I don't want no money." It was no use. I didn't love him.

I said to my friend, "I don't want him." She said, "What? He's your fiancé. He sent money to New York for a ring. He's not a dress you can change and get another one." I said, "Listen, I don't love him. That's all." I took off the ring and gave it back to him.

I used to love to dress up and go to parties. One day, I went to a party with my sisters and saw a boy playing a mandolin and singing. I said to my sister, "You know, he has a beautiful song." The next day, my sister was married. He came to the wedding. All of a sudden, he came to me and said, "I want to have a nice girl. The first time I saw you, I was after you." I said, "Why don't you tell me before?" He said, "I was afraid maybe you were going to refuse, but now is the time—tonight is a wedding night. I want you." So I got engaged the same day my sister got married.

He gave me a wonderful life.

He died seven years ago, but I'm not going to get married again. I went to Jerusalem and a man said, "My wife died. I want to get married." I said, "No." I went to Rhodes to visit somebody who says, "Get married. Find a good man." I said, "Listen, honey, I don't want to get married again. I won't find a husband like my husband. Never."

I'm always thinking of him. When he was sick from his stroke, he said, "You work too hard." I said, "No, don't tell me that. I am your wife. You are my husband. I didn't get married the way you are now. I am looking at you with the same eyes, just like I saw you the first time." He smiled and we kissed each other. He was an angel.

When he died, the doctor said, "Change your furniture around. Paint your rooms different colors to not think so much about him all the time." I didn't do it. I look at the chair he used to sit in. It seems like he is sitting there still, and we are having coffee together again.

Lou Pilisuk (narrated by his wife, Charlotte)

Austria and Russia

I met Lou when he was about nineteen. It was in a park, a beautiful day. He was spontaneous, warm, and friendly. He didn't care that I was deaf. He'd just say to me, "If you want to hear, you will." So I began to listen more and it helped me.

Lou has difficulty speaking because of the Parkinson's, so I'll tell you the story from what he told me when we were younger. He was born in Austria, the middle of three children. Right after he was born, his family moved to Russia. When he was two years old, his father was killed by a Cossack soldier. He was crossing a bridge and a soldier on horseback called out, "Stop or I'll shoot." So he stopped. The soldier asked where he lived and he told him. Then the soldier said, "I'll take you home." He tied his foot to the horse's foot and dragged him all the way home in the snow. When he arrived home, he developed pneumonia and died in three days.

So Lou, his brother, sister, and widowed mother went to live with the grandmother in her one-room hut. It had a thatched roof and they used to plug it up tight in the cold weather with rags. Lou used to say, the part he remembers most is when his mother left for America. She went in a horse and wagon and all the family watched her go, wagging handkerchiefs and crying.

It took at least a year for his mother to raise enough money to send for the rest of the family. In the meantime, she met a man and was remarried. Her husband told her that he couldn't support her whole family, so Lou had to go to an orphan home in New York when he was seven years old. He lived there until he was fifteen, when he ran away. It was a terrible place. They didn't have enough shoes or clothes or food. The boys were not fed. When he was fifteen, his supervisor punched him in the nose and made it bleed. Lou said, "That's it. I'm leaving and I'm leaving right now. I don't want a thing from you." So he walked to his mother's house in the Bronx, quite a ways away, and his stepfather answered the door. He said, "What are you doing here? I can't provide for you." But they let him stay because he worked. He brought an income into the family.

We were married in 1929. Lou was very smart. He had been one of the leading scholars at the *Yeshiva* in the orphan home. So I encouraged him to go to school. He worked until very late in a demanding job and went to school at night. When our second son was born, he got his high school diploma.

When both of our sons graduated from college, Lou said, "I want to go too." He was so tired. He said, "I've been working since I was fourteen. First I supported my mother and then I supported my family. I want to retire and go to school." So he made the decision and went to Queen's College in New York where both our sons went.

He wasn't able to finish because he got sick with Parkinson's when he was sixty-two. We went from neurologist to neurologist, from specialist to specialist. We even lived in Florida for a while. Everyone feels better in the sunshine, but it didn't help the Parkinson's.

In 1974, a couple years later, we moved to Seattle to be near one of our sons. Lou's condition is getting worse, but I'll keep him at home as long as I can. He always wants to help. Yesterday I had a cold and he came by and covered my feet. He is very devoted. How can you put someone like that away.

One night he started to cry. He felt like such a burden. So I started to cry too. Then I said, "We've laughed together, so now we'll cry together. We'll laugh together again."

Harry Policar

Isle of Marmara

Our daughter who lives by the water said, "All our neighbors have totem poles. Why don't you carve us some?" What do I know about carving totem poles? I never carved one in my life. So on my birthday they give me some tools and I went for a couple of semesters here at the high school at night to learn. I did a few masks, some seagulls.

Now I garden, play a little golf, do a lot of fishing. Fishing for me is easy. I go down to the water and get in the boat. I started all my grandchildren fishing, and they love it too. We like fish like we used to eat them in Marmara, baked or broiled, nothing to ruin the taste. In Marmara, if you didn't like fish, you starved. That's all.

The Isle of Marmara had about six villages. The town of Marmara had about two thousand people, the majority Greeks. There must have been about twenty-five Jewish families there, and the same number of Turkish families. The other five villages were all Greek.

In 1492 when the Jews were expelled from Spain, the Turkish government accepted about fifty thousand Jews in Turkey. The Jews all went to Istanbul, a big city. It was hard for them to make a living after a while because the Jewish people were practically all in the same kind of businesses. So they started to scatter all over Turkey. A few went to Marmara. We were the ones that went: my great-great-grandfather. It was a place to make a living. We weren't bothered by the government.

We could do what we wanted until the First World War. My grandfather and father were both bakers. During the war, they took the Greeks out of Marmara and sent all inland (like they did here with the Japanese during the Second World War), because the Greeks were fighting against the Turks at the time, and the Turks felt the Greeks on Marmara might get together with the enemy.

With the Greeks gone, Marmara was nothing there. We stayed as long as we could. Finally I came to this country because my father said, "You have to go. There's no future for young boys here." At that time I was about to be drafted into the Turkish army.

I never saw my father again. I was seventeen when I left Marmara in 1920. That's when everybody was coming over. They wanted to forget and get away from that misery we had.

I had two uncles that were in Seattle, my mother's brother and my father's brother. My father had been here in 1909. He stayed for a couple years, made a

couple thousand dollars, thought he'd made a fortune, so came back to Turkey to retire. He said to me before I left, "Go to Seattle. It's like Marmara, surrounded by water, and we have relatives there."

When I came to New York, I didn't even have a suitcase with me. I had an oud, a Turkish instrument I used to play when I was a kid. It's on my piano now. That's all I had in my hand and the clothes I had on. I had fifty cents to my name. There was a Greek boy on the ship, a neighbor of mine from Marmara. He said, "Harry, how much money you got?" I said, "Fifty cents." He said, "Where you gonna go?" I said, "I don't know. I'm going to stay in New York." "Well," he said, "can you loan me twenty-five cents?" He was completely broke. He wanted to go the Greek district. So here I was in Ellis Island with twenty-five cents.

An interpreter came and talked with me. He asked where I was going. I said I'd like to go to Seattle but didn't have any money. He said, "Haven't you got any friends around here that might have money?" I went up to two girls I know from Marmara—their name was Policar, not related to me. I said, "Hey girls, got any money?" They said they had lots of money. I borrowed the fare to Seattle from them, twenty dollars, and that's how I got to Seattle. So this man went to the window and got my ticket for me.

It took most people a couple years to scrape and save to come to this country. The fare was only about twenty dollars to cross the Atlantic, but nobody had that money. They had to save pennies and nickels and everything they had.

In Seattle I went to work for the same family in the bakery business my father had worked for when he was here. After that, I worked in another large bakery for forty years, superintendent for about thirty-five years. I sent my brothers and my sister in Turkey some money from here, but they couldn't come to this country because of a very strict Turkish quota by that time. They went instead to Cuba, thinking they'd be close to this country, but they had to wait ten years to come here.

I retired in 1972, ten years ago. I still bake all the time, everything that I can think of. A couple of weeks ago I wanted croissants. I never made croissants, but I made some, and now everybody wants to learn how to make them. When the ladies are talking about baking, they get me in the conversation because I'm the only one in the gang that knows about it.

Hanna Povlsen

Austria

Only once have I seen war from close up: in Iran when the Russians came and the Germans had to get out. The bombs fell where I lived, but it was far enough away so the people came out of their houses to watch. It was not something you see every day. The airplanes were small and one person could die. Now if there is a war, there is no future for anybody.

Our family left Austria before the war, in 1938. It was because of my mother. She had a rotten imagination and knew what was going to happen. She didn't see gas chambers, of course—who could see that? But she knew the Jews would be killed. She was very impatient for us to leave the country, but my father didn't want to leave. He was innocent. He felt Vienna was his home. My mother had to work on him and it took him a long time, almost too long, before he agreed to leave. By that time, the situation was intolerable. Jews would disappear and come back in a coffin.

I was twenty-eight when our family left, and engaged to a man in Denmark. One of my brothers was already in Denmark so I joined him and my fiancé there. My other brother went to Ireland and my parents went to Sweden.

After my husband and I were married, we moved to Iran where he was working as a civil engineer for a Danish company. It was not hard to be Jewish in Iran in 1939. Nothing happened to us. But then, the Germans were in Egypt and it was very close, so the Danish Consulate prepared the Danes to leave. They prepared us, but they didn't help us. We learned that embassies and consulates are hard to deal with.

One day the consulate told us an American missionary was going back to America. I came to him and told him that I am expecting a baby and could he help us to America on his boat. He was so nice, so warm, so more than I could expect. He said he could

help us. We sold everything we had and my husband gave up his job. We went to where we should meet the missionary and go on the boat to America. When we got there, he had forgotten everything about our meeting a few weeks before. He said, "How could I possibly take anyone who is expecting a baby?" So we went back to Tehran, my husband got another job, we got our old apartment back, and we stayed there a year and a half longer.

Because it was wartime, it was difficult for a civilian to find transportation to America. We finally got a visa but we had no transportation. So we went to India to wait for a ship to America. We lived two months in Bombay. We were like tourists, in a boarding house.

One day we had a telephone call that a boat is leaving the next morning for America. It was so sudden—my little boy's diapers were in the water and we packed them wet. The boat we were on was a troop-transport ship carrying only missionaries and us. The first few days we were escorted by warships, but then we were on the free ocean and nothing happened to us. We arrived in Los Angeles in 1944, waited a few days, and then went on the train to Seattle. My mother was in Seattle waiting for us.

I started working very late in life. I was trained as a teacher in Vienna, but I didn't get much time to work. When I was fifty years old, I started teaching again. It was my chance. I taught German and kindergarten in a private school. I retired about twelve years later, and now I'm afraid I don't do enough. My time is filled up, but I think one has to do more.

I'm very much concerned about what is going on in this world. I'd like to do more for the peace movement, for the arms freeze. I will take part in a peace march next week with my husband. He sometimes has difficulty walking, but it is important to go. When we are tired, we will stop.

Rose Pruzan

Russia

When I left Russia to come to America with my little baby, I didn't know where I was going. I'm not educated. My husband was in America and he sent for us. But he didn't send a passport for the baby so I had to smuggle her over the border. I traveled in a wagon with all men and when we got to the border, it was five o'clock in the morning and a blizzard. My baby was crying so hard because she was hungry and cold. I had her wrapped up in a blanket and she slipped out into the snow. My baby was lying in the snow and she got frozen there. Some people came to help me and we had to stick needles in her and put her hands in cold water. And I was fainting. I'll never forget it.

In Liverpool I got robbed at the immigration station. I was sleeping and somebody took all my money. I woke up crying and a man came over to me and said, "I'm Jewish. Would you like I should treat you for breakfast or lunch? Give me the baby and we'll go." I said, "Oh no." I wouldn't dare give him the baby. I held the baby tight to my heart.

When I got to Boston, they examined me and sent a letter to my husband, telling him I got robbed and he should send me money to buy some food on the train. I had to change trains every three days with my baby to get to Seattle from Boston. I didn't trust nobody. I didn't have any food for six days. Anybody who left their seat on the train, I walked over, and if there was any part of a sandwich, I ate it. I didn't care if it was ham. I was hungry. Except for that, my baby and me lived on water. I was so scared.

When I got to Seattle, my husband didn't recognize me because I was so skinny and dirty. Then he took me to his sister's house and I took a bath and put on clean clothes and she made the most wonderful dinner. Everything was ready for me. When we got there, I was so happy I kissed the sidewalk.

My husband was very good to me. I had five children right here in this country. My husband wants boys so I had three sons and three daughters. All the cooking and baking and washing I did! We didn't have much money so I made everything from potatoes. Potato soup, potato latkes, potato pancakes. My husband would look at me and say, "You're wonderful."

I love to remember all the things that happened to me in my life. For a minute I can remember everything . . . then I forget. It's my age. A lot of people, when they're old, they don't want to tell their age. They're afraid for something. I say, "What's to be afraid? You're here today, you're gone tomorrow. Nobody knows when it's coming." I'm ninety-three years old and I still do all the baking and the cooking. Anything you would want. I say to people, "My name is Rose Pruzan. If you come to me, I'm not going to give you a piece of bread, I'm going to give you three pieces bread," because that's the way I am, all my life.

Alfred Püchler

Czechoslovakia and Austria

I believe very much in God. I am not very religious but I go every week to the synagogue. I keep the holidays. Whatever I do, I know it is God's willing.

When they need me, I work at the Jewish Federation, on the Jewish newspaper, and in Jewish education. I never was an office worker, but the hours I spend stuffing envelopes in these offices now are better than any medication.

Otherwise I go with friends sometimes for lunch, and relatives invite me for dinner. A professional German cook, a lady from Munich, also makes food for me. Every two weeks, she comes for six hours and cooks whatever I want. People tell me I should learn to cook, but I don't want to—not a whole meal.

I am going to be eighty-two, but I don't believe it. I was born Christmas Eve, 1900, in Czechoslovakia. I came to Vienna when I was eight. I couldn't speak one word of German, but the teacher forbid me to speak Czechoslovakian, so I had to learn it quickly. I had to go to work when I was fourteen because my father passed away when I was ten. After that I went to night school.

In Vienna I had my Bar Mitzvah, my education, and my marriage in 1935. Hitler came and in 1939, I was taken to a labor camp in Poland. He drafted the youth from eighteen to forty-five to establish occupied land there. Four thousand men went by train we didn't know where. Eighty percent of the Jews were doctors, lawyers, intellectuals, but for the camps, the working people were called—the carpenters, electricians, a few architects. Not too many Jewish people had trades, but I myself was a house painter because I thought it would be easier to emigrate with a trade.

In Poland they started shooting. At first we had to sleep in the bunkhouses of the Polish farmers. For three weeks we didn't change our clothes. Then we started building barracks, crude barracks, which took two or three months. The Polish farmers, the non-Jews, were surprised to see Jewish people working so hard. "You cannot be Jewish," they said.

In 1941 before Purim, there was a rumor that we, people from Vienna and the rest from Czechoslovakia, would be sent home. In Yiddish we said, "We're going home," and then the SS commander of the whole camp told us we'd be returned to Vienna and would have to emigrate immediately.

By this time my wife was in hiding. In Vienna I had to report right away to the Gestapo. Eichmann was there. They said, "In three weeks you have to leave the country." We still had a visa to South America. My wife's whole family was already there. But it was not possible—the harbor was already closed.

My wife had a brother in Shanghai. Our only possibility was to go there, through Siberia. The arrangements were very difficult. We sold everything we had. Finally we had only four dollars and a little bag.

In June 1941 we finally arrived. There were about fifteen thousand refugees in Shanghai. When we arrived there, we lived in a school building, eight couples in a room, almost a year. The climate in summer was sometimes 120 degrees, food was rationed, and we had to report to the Japanese. Almost every day when the war started, the Americans bombed Shanghai.

Finally we found a little room in a Chinese house. I was working as a salesman for a Chinese company selling paper bags and old newspaper to the meat markets and little grocery stores. My wife was helping too. We just survived.

When the war ended in 1945, we could hardly believe it. I had a sister in Seattle. She sent us an affidavit. In 1947 we went by military transport ship, the *General Migs*. We had bunks three high, but water we could drink.

After three days here, a friend of mine recommended me to work in a factory. I made Christmas tree sets, seventy-five cents an hour, very hard work, but I was happy. One day the boss came and said, "Alfred, tomorrow you're working in the shipping department, $1.36 an hour and seven days." I'll never forget it. I had to join the union. I still get my news, Teamster, Local 130. I never did that kind of work, but I learned.

I worked until I was sixty-five and then retired. I started drawing, doing other work, but I was not really happy. A gentleman who had a men's furnishings wholesale business gave me a job, but at seventy-three, I said, "That's it."

Now comes the sad part of my story. My wife passed away four years ago. Inside, I am *zerbrochen*, broken. We had the happiest marriage, lived together in the best harmony in the world. Now I can cry any time, thinking of her. They say, "A man should not cry." Why should a man not cry? It depends on what kind of feeling you have in you. My wife is waiting for me.

Leon Rousso

Isle of Rhodes

I was born a long time ago, November 1898. I had a big family. I lost them all. My father died when I was five years old. At that time we didn't have no pictures to see what he looked like. We didn't believe in pictures, almost eighty years ago. My mother worked hard to raise the family. I came to the United States in 1916. I brought my mother and my youngest brother over in 1919.

The Isle of Rhodes was very pretty. One of the seven wonders of the world. I was there in 1973 to see my house. The same house was still there. I never thought it would be like that, the same as when I left. In my time there used to be lots of farmers in the Isle of Rhodes. After so many years, they find out there is no money in that. So they build houses, jewelry stores, fur stores, big business. They don't care for farming any more. When we were there in 1973, we saw the olives. They were all dry and on the ground.

We need the farmers. I started working in the market after school when I first came to this country. I had my own stall for fifty years, fruits and vegetables. In the old times, my wife used to help me down there. I had no trouble with the people. I like people all the time.

They were good to me. I was good to them. I mind my own business. I sold my place about eight years ago, but I still go there to work a couple times a week. A lot of people come to the market. I got a lot of friends at the market. When they see me, they yell, "Rousso! Rousso! Rousso!"

I'm the oldest Jew in the market, the oldest of the old timers.

Abraham Sambol

Poland

In the Austrian part of Poland, Jews were mostly merchants, tailors, and shoemakers. Every week the Jewish merchants from small towns would come to my city, Rzeszow, and buy manufactured goods. They would come in horse and wagon to buy supplies for the peasants—whatever a peasant needs. My father had an unusual occupation for a Jew. He worked in a steel factory. He worked hard, twelve hours a day. Ten hours in the factory and two hours at home, doing repairs for people on their things that went on the blink. But with all that, he could hardly make ends meet. So in 1922 he left for America. He became a citizen after five years and sent for us, my mother and four children. I was the oldest, twenty years old.

When I got to New York, I had to find work. In Poland I was working lugging the bales of goods the merchants bought in our city. But in New York, there was no horse and wagon so I didn't have a trade. There was nothing to do but paint. Painting was a Jewish, German, and Swedish trade. My second brother and I started our own painting business. In 1929 my third brother started working with us. When I went to estimate a job, I was always shooting too low. I got the jobs, but we didn't make any money. My younger brother, he was Americanized, and he was always shooting too high. He never got the jobs. My middle brother was shooting in the middle. We decided to make him manager. After a while my brother got married. He was dividing the work between us for the week three ways. I knew he had a family to support, so I said, "Why should you divide the work between the three of us? You can use the extra days. Where I would really like to be is in Palestine, working on a kibbutz."

I felt a compulsion to work on the land, to work in a vineyard. It was in my blood. On my father's side, they were all farmers. In 1934 I went to Israel. I stayed in Tel Aviv for a few weeks before I went to the kibbutz. About twenty-five of my friends from Poland were there in Tel Aviv. No one ever locked their door. My friends would be at work. I'd let myself in

and read the paper until they came home. The policemen, the firemen, everybody was Jewish. Even the street cleaners with their sidelocks. Everybody was so friendly. I used to come into the stores where they sold butter, milk, cheese. One day, as soon as I walked in, I gave my order. Give me this and this and this. And the owner says, "Where's your good morning?" You used to be able to rent half a room or a quarter of a room. No one minded living that way. When you sleep, you sleep. You didn't worry your possessions will disappear. I went on to the kibbutz and I fit in like a glove. In the vineyards we worked ten hours a day but those hours passed before I even looked around. In the wintertime, when it poured, if there was only work for one man, I was out there.

I would have never come back, but after three years I got a letter from America that my mother was sick with cancer. I came back to see her, but she only lived one week. After six months I wanted to go back to Israel, but my passport expired. The consulate wouldn't give me a renewal because I was military age. So I got stuck here. I got married and worked as a painter again.

My wife passed away young, with cancer, so I went back to Israel after I retired. This time I lived in Tel Aviv. I was too old to be on the kibbutz. They didn't want me. What could I do? When I was in Tel Aviv the second time, everything was different. It became New Yorkized. No more renting half a room. You want an apartment, you go to a real estate agent and he gets a commission. I couldn't afford to live there anymore. After five years I came back to America. I didn't leave Israel, Israel left me.

Still, Israel is a part of me. From living on the kibbutz, I don't need many possessions. I'm used to living sparse. Nothing would please me more than to move from the city and live on a farm. I like the outside. But I don't for one reason and one reason only. I must have Jews. There are no Jews in the country.

Hazel Saperstein

Russia

I was born in Libau, Russia, in 1893. Libau was a beautiful city, right on the seacoast, peaceful, with beer gardens and streets lined with palm trees. All of our family was there, aunts and uncles too. My father was a tailor and manufactured clothes at home. It was just like a factory and he would hire people to work for him there.

We were five sisters in my family. We came to America when we were just young children. I was eight years old.

How we came here is a fairy tale, really. My grandmother had a brother who disappeared when he was fourteen years old. He never even said good-bye. My grandmother mourned him and thought she would never see him again. Fifty years later she got a letter from him. In his letter, he couldn't apologize enough for the heartache he had caused her and said he would make up for it all. He said, "I'm a rich man in America and I want you all to come here." Gradually, a little at a time, the whole family came to America. We were on a small wooden ship and it tossed and turned . . . we thought we would never reach London. We were in the steerage with the animals for about eight days. After we reached England we got on a big ship. We landed in New York first and they kept us about two weeks in the immigration station. We went from New York to Tacoma where my great-uncle lived. He was there waiting for us.

In Tacoma I went to school where I had to be in the baby class because I didn't know the language. I graduated from the eighth grade and then learned from life and from my family. Education isn't everything. It's character that counts.

I lived with my parents until I got married. I was twenty-one or twenty-two. Now there are children and grandchildren and great-grandchildren. At my age, I don't have much of a future but I have a great past to think about. Everything I want to remember— it's all inside me.

When I was younger and my papa would come to see me, I'd say, "How do you feel today, Papa?" And he'd say, "I feel like an old man." And I'd say, "I don't know, how does an old man feel?" And Papa would say, "An old man feels like a woman in her ninth month and expecting any day." And his words are true. I could be in my ninth month.

I am already a year older than my great-uncle was when he passed away. He lived to be eighty-six years old, and the day he passed away was the greatest day of his life. As he lay in his bed, all the family he had brought over surrounded him, thanking him for what he had done. If he hadn't brought us to America, Hitler would have destroyed us all.

Max Schoenfeld

Germany

I was fourteen years old when we came to the United States in 1896 from Germany—I've been working ever since. We lived in Wabash, Indiana, first and I worked right away making boxes in a hat factory. I made three and a half cents an hour, working ten hours a day. The next year we moved to Chicago and I worked for my uncle in the clothing business. This time I made four dollars a week, and I must have worked ten hours a day, six days a week. I had to pay sixty cents car fare out of it and by the time I had lunches, there wasn't much left. I worked in that business ten years.

We moved to Seattle in 1907. I was a traveling salesman, selling ties wholesale from store to store. I went to small towns and big cities. It was hard work. One time, in Montana, it was fifty-five below zero and the wind was blowing about fifty miles an hour. We didn't have cars before 1910, so I had to travel by walking, train, and horse and buggy.

I met my wife in Seattle. It was July 3, 1923. She was from Chicago and visiting an aunt. She went back to Chicago the latter part of July and we corresponded. In November we got engaged. I went to New York on a business trip and stopped in Chicago to give her the ring. When I was in New York I was busy every minute. I couldn't call her, so I sent her a postcard that said, "I'm going to be in Chicago Saturday morning. As soon as I get there, I'll call you and you'd better come downtown so we can get our marriage license." When I got to the courthouse, I called her and she came right down. She told me later that she was sore to think I wouldn't take more time than just sending her a postcard. But we've been happily married for fifty-eight years.

These days I still go to work. I never give it a thought—being one hundred years old. I just go along from day to day. A boy from the office picks me up every morning and brings me home in the afternoon. There's not much to do anymore, but I enjoy being with people. I don't like to stay home—the time gets too long. You know, there's no use talking . . . when you get older, you're not the same. There are changes. Up until two years ago I played golf. I could hit the ball just as good as I did thirty years ago. Then one day I was bending over and I felt my back go out. I've had to quit playing golf, but I'll do a little putting when the weather gets nice. I always find something to do.

To live to be one hundred, act natural. Do what you want, but don't overdo. Be reasonable and use a little judgment. Stay active. That's what I do, all the time.

Irving Seidman

Russia

I'm going to Israel next week to plant trees for my mother's memory. Maybe I'll put up a monument. She was killed trying to save me when I was a small boy. There was a revolution going on and our town was in the middle of it. Every day a different troop would come through. A General Denikin had an army that was fighting the Bolsheviks. They were on their way to the Polish border, and in the meantime, robbing and burning and killing. One day they came to our house. My father didn't want to let them in, but they said if he wouldn't open the door, they would come in the window. I got scared—a young boy— and let them in. The first thing they did was pull off my boots. Then a soldier told me to dig up the money. We were poor, we didn't have any money so the soldier got mad and started hitting me with his rifle. I was crying and hollering because it hurt.

My mother ran over to me and grabbed the rifle and he shot her dead. Luckily he didn't have any more bullets to kill the rest of the family so we were able to run out of the house. We ran in the snow for three days. Every time I talk about it, I can't help it, I start to cry. But I'm still alive, and I'm healthy.

When I was eighteen, I came to America. It was time to start making a living for myself. My brother was already here and had a cleaning and laundry business in Greenwich Village, New York. I couldn't speak any English, so he taught me how to iron shirts. I became a shirt ironer. In June, July, and August, I was sweating like anything and when the drops fell on a shirt, I went over them with the iron. I produced ninety or more shirts a day. And I earned good money, thirty-five to thirty-eight dollars a week, in 1922.

When I had some money saved, I decided to go to Europe and see my girl friend. I knew her before— she was a distant relative. I stayed there three months until my money ran out and then came back to America. After a few months, she finally came here too.

When I was tired of working in the laundry, I started working in the fur trade. I had to soak and stretch and cut out the damage on rabbit fur. I did that three or four months and then lost my job because of some trouble in the union. After that I opened up my own cleaning and laundry. I was there three or four years until my ex-wife came up with the idea of a day school. She was a genius. She read a book about a nursery school, so we decided to open one up in Newark, New Jersey. I would pick up the kids every morning in a big car, sometimes twenty or more of them, and I remember I had to rush in the snow because they were waiting outside. I love children. I'm crazy about them whether they are mine or not. We had the school for some years. It was a good living.

After that, my wife stayed in Newark and I went on to Los Angeles. But I didn't like it there. The young people, they act like western cowboys riding their cars. So I came to Seattle. It was like a small town with the signs faded on the streets. And I liked the weather. In Newark, you sweat like anything in the summer and it's humid. I had to sleep in the basement. Here, you cover yourself with a blanket in June. It's God's country. I'm here already thirty-two years.

You know, there are many widows these days. In my opinion, the reason is, they don't have to hit their husbands with their fists, they kill them with their mouths. Mrs. Seidman and I are married now for nine years. I was alone for a long time, so I decided to marry this sweetheart. When it comes to women, she is an angel. If a wife is good to her husband and gives him some credit, he will live a long time. I'm seventy-nine and still going strong.

Jenny Spitzer

Austria

Austria is famous for Mozart and the Strauss family. I was born in Vienna in 1887. Around the turn of the century was the high point in musical life in Vienna. When we were young, we went to the opera house. We would stand or sit on the inexpensive seats and listen to our heart's delight. For young people it was a great thing.

We had a very big family at home. I was the oldest of six children. My father would take me along everywhere he went. He was a mountain lover. My mother would stay at home with the children and my father took me to Germany and the Netherlands. We had a wonderful time together.

My mother kept me apart from boys. We were not free with young men and boys like here in America. I started to have a young girl's life when I was already twenty or older. I married and lived with my husband in Vienna until 1938. We had a son and a daughter.

We were a sportive family. My children inherited it from us. The whole family liked the mountains. My husband and I were pioneer skiers. We had a lively, happy life—outings and holidays and weekends to the mountains.

Then came Hitler. At first we were not worried. My husband thought, "Well, we are older people, they won't harm us." Then things were getting worse and worse. At that time my daughter was married to a Swiss man and lived in Zurich. My boy was on a traveling tour and was also in Switzerland. He called us one night and my husband said, "Don't come home with this terrible cold. Please don't come home." My son knew what he meant—don't come home to the arms of Hitler. So we knew at least we didn't have to worry about our children.

In March of 1938 Hitler swallowed Austria. Things got very bad but we still had time to leave. It was not easy, but my son-in-law got us a visa to Switzerland. The last day in Vienna, December 18, 1938, it was our anniversary. We thought what we could do special for this day—before the train. We went over to one of the nice bourgeois restaurants and had a dinner to our taste, very Viennese. Mushroom soup and boiled meat and a good dessert. No drinks. I remember it well. The Nazis took everything away from us but twenty dollars, but we were lucky to get out.

We went to Switzerland. My daughter and son-in-law had gone to Seattle. They decided to stay in Seattle because there they were free. She wrote to my husband and me and said, "For one year we will leave our very nice apartment in Zurich to you." This was in 1941. Then the war broke out and Switzerland was closed until 1945. We were not allowed to work because we were foreigners. Our son-in-law supported us.

After the war we decided to come to America. We came to Seattle in 1946. My husband was too old to make a living anymore so I started with all kinds of little things—babysitting and fancywork, crocheting, and knitting.

My husband died in 1951. Time passed and I got older and older and older. My life was a very quiet one. When people want stories about the immigrants, they feel they have to hear of murder and suffering. Well, we lost things—our property and our money. But we didn't lose each other so I can't complain. We always had each other.

Samuel Steinberg

Russia

Relatives that lived in big cities used to come to our *shtetl* Shamki like they come for a vacation. We had a garden and the forest. It was a beautiful place. We came from a town of about sixty families. Before 1850, eight families bought the land under a certain czar that allowed Jews to buy land. Over there, everybody lived in one place like a street or two streets. The land was in three sections. One place was for rye, one for potatoes, one for oats and barley and stuff like that. Potatoes were the only thing that we had a surplus, and we used to sell in the fall to the next town that had a brewery. They used to make vodka out of the potatoes. After we got the money, the shoemaker came and made shoes for everybody. The only thing we needed actually to buy was salt, sugar, kerosene, sometimes herring. Everybody had enough food. Food we had.

From the sixty families we had, four were Christians because you've got to have somebody to do the work Saturdays, like milk the cows. One of our townspeople went to a big city once to see a relative. So on the train he met another Jew from a big town. "How many Jews, how many Christians do you got in your town Shamki?" the stranger wanted to know. "Oh, about sixty families, four Christian." The man said in his town there were twenty thousand Christians. "What do you do with so many?" the man from Shamki wanted to know. In Russia I thought we were the head . . .

My father was an expert in cucumbers. We raised a lot of them and we used to sell them. They had to be selected, you know, perfect, very good. We used to get for sixty, fifteen cents. Those days, you know. And some people didn't have the fifteen cents where we used to sell them in the other town, so they gave me, instead of a penny, an egg. The egg was worth a little more than a cent, so it was better if they didn't have the money.

In our town we had no post office. We used to go to the next town about four miles away. A regular city I was about eleven years old. I used to run fast and pick up the mail for the whole town, maybe ten pieces of mail. Once, when I came in the post office, there was a picture of the czar on the wall. So the

officer points me to the picture. He tells me in Russian, "*Shopka.*" That means a hat. I didn't know what he meant, a hat. So there was another Jewish fellow. He said, "Take off your hat when you see the picture of the czar." He said, "It's a good thing you are small. Otherwise, he would give you a beating."

Our town had a synagogue, and we had about three people that were teaching the children. We had a Rabbi and a *shochet*, a butcher that killed the cattle. We had like a teacher that was mostly teaching studies like Hebrew, the Bible, the Talmud, but then, towards the end, one man, a Christian, came and opened a school to teach Russian. I knew how to write Russian, but there was nobody to talk to in Russian. The Christians in our town spoke Yiddish.

A brother of my father's came to America and wrote a letter back. He wrote it in Hebrew. His business he describes that he deals in copper, in iron, in old clothes. So my father thought he must be a very wealthy millionaire. In Hebrew it sounds big—iron for lead. So he came here and saw his brother was just a peddler.

When we came here in 1910, we lived on Main Street. Now they call it slums. We didn't call it slums. We had no furnace. A rich man had a furnace! My mother used to take a dollar—we were a family of seven—and we used to eat very well. A sack of potatoes, one hundred pounds for a dollar, from a peddler. Go to the butcher and buy three pounds meat for thirty cents. We didn't consider we lived in slums.

Eventually our family got into the wholesale business so Saturday was not in the way. I'm now mostly retired. I am actually supposed to be retired but I don't like to stay home. I come here eight in the morning on the bus. Here I have a lot of work to do—open the mail in the morning and distribute it to the different people, the local mail, the eastern mail. Then I check invoices. Now they make invoices on the computer. The computer probably doesn't make mistakes but sometimes you punch the wrong key so you got to check every invoice. I keep busy.

I was born in 1893. Next September I'll be eightynine. There are not too many people alive now who came here before me.

Jeannette Sterling

Turkey

I was born in Turkey. My father was from Poland and my mother was from Russia. They started killing the Jews in both places but my parents heard Turkey was good to the Jews, so they decided to go there.

On Saturdays Momma would take us children down to the waterfront. They had the best sandwiches there—Swiss cheeses, the real thing.

My father was the first to leave the old country. He was a very famous pants maker. He made pants for the sultan of Turkey. He saved up some money and when he arrived in New York, he got room and board with a family. They told him to go in and take a bath. Well he went in there and he never came out. They said in Jewish, "For goodness' sakes, what's the matter with you? Are you alive or what?" He was waiting for the water to cool off. He didn't know that in America you could run hot and cold water at the same time.

He made enough money to fix up a little home and sent for Momma, the children, and Grandma. I came over with my aunt and my grandfather when I was eight years old. We took a boat from Turkey to France, steerage. We slept on top of the deck. I can just see the waves now, those green-blue waves almost to the top of the boat. And seasick . . . Oy, God!

We stopped at the immigration station, or Castle Garden as it was called then. Oh, it was filthy there. They didn't want to let us into America because my grandfather's eyes were bad. My aunt was talking to an official and I walked over to see what's going on. My auntie says to me, "Vein! Vein!" (Cry! Cry!) So we both cried. Oy, I cried my eyes out and what for I didn't know. She told me to cry so I cried. It worked. They let us through, thank God.

Then we went on the train to Seattle, Washington. We pronounced it "Settlevash." When we got to Seattle we were all sitting together, a lot of immigrants with their bundles. There was a committee that came down to meet us. They said, "Well, where are you going?"

We said, "We're going to Settlevash."

They said, "Get off the train. This is Seattle, Washington."

And we said, "No, we're going to Settlevash." We wouldn't budge.

From Seattle we went to Alaska where my relatives had a general store. The Indians took me to them in a canoe. I kept looking for a city. In Alaska we lived three or four miles from a school. I had a Husky dog and I trained him to pull me to school on a sled. I had the hardest time teaching him to pull me because when I'd call his name, he'd come to me. I couldn't make him understand to go ahead. Then the Indians came along with their sled of females and he would follow the females. That's how he learned to pull me.

I lived in Alaska eight years and then came to Seattle and I met my husband. We got married and we lived together sixty-one years. He passed away two years ago. That's the story and here I am in a nursing home. I didn't want to burden my son. Altogether I couldn't stay alone anymore. I'll tell you, when you have a husband, you're somebody. If you become a widow . . . people have their own lives. They're busy. Home I was sitting alone. Here I see people.

It reminds me of a story. There was a traveling salesman who had to go on business trips. He was selling merchandise. First he used to take his wife with him, but she got tired of travel. So she stayed home. Finally one time she couldn't take it so she says to him, "I don't want you to go on trips anymore. I can't stand to be alone. All I do all day is stare at the four walls."

So he says to her, "You're right, honey. You know what I'm going to do for you? I'm going to build you another wall."

Gustave Stern

Germany

It's getting lost so fast. If no one asks me things like this, I don't even think of them. . . .

On the twentieth of February, 1982, it was forty years since we came on the ship from Marseilles. We lived in Germany until 1933, when we moved—moved, that's a joke—Hitler was after us. It's such a big story, I could tell it for hours, hours, hours. In 1933 after I had lost my profession as opera conductor, we moved first to Holland and then to Paris where we lived for over nine years.

My parents who still lived in Germany wanted to visit my uncle, my father's brother, in Fargo, North Dakota, so they went to see him in 1938. When they came back, they visited us in Paris, and my father was in an accident. He was run over by a truck and broke his leg, so they couldn't go back to Germany. In the meantime was the infamous Crystal Night. After that, we would not let them go back. They had with them only the suitcases they had taken with them to America.

My uncle from Fargo eventually brought to this country over a hundred and ten families from Germany. When his finances ran out, he went even to the governor of North Dakota. He brought us over, too. We received our visas on the day when Roosevelt declared war on Hitler. We heard it in the office in Marseilles, and we were the last ones to get out with our visas. We came on a big chartered ship, only for refugees. On the twentieth of February, 1942, we arrived in New York. It was very cold. My two sons were sick.

We stayed in New York four weeks, then moved to Chicago, but it was too windy and too hot. We went for a year and a half to Fargo. Again it was windy and hot, and I was discontented because I was not in the profession I wanted to be. I sold suits, and I didn't like that. I also came just a little back into music—I gave lessons, and was the organist in a Congregational church.

My uncle in Fargo always said, "If I would be young, I would go to Seattle." So we went to Seattle. When we came here, my father was sick. He had a cancer operation and he wanted a German-speaking doctor. Some people from our home town recommended a doctor. One evening the doctor came and I met him for the first time. I was very much in a hurry. I wanted to go to a concert. "You are musical?" he says. "I'm a bit musical too. What do you play? The piano? You have to come tomorrow night to our place."

So I went and played the piano and had a good steak, and after he heard me, he called some people immediately. They came over the same evening. It just so happened that at the Civic Opera, they were looking for a conductor, and I became their conductor. I conducted my first opera in Seattle in 1946, *Die Fledermaus*.

Through the doctor I met someone from Seattle University. I started to teach there—voice lessons, German. Everything started to click.

We rehearsed the operas in the field house which belonged to the city. One Sunday afternoon a couple came to me and the man said, "I'm the new superintendent of parks; I'm very interested in music, and I want to revitalize the music in the parks. The man had plans and money. I accepted. We did Mozart, we did everything. We even did *Aida* in the park!

Everything was just luck. My grandfather used to say a nail's full of luck is worth a whole arm of intelligence.

Eventually the neighborhoods changed. They wanted hippie music, not classical. In 1970 I retired.

Some people say, "Oh, I cannot do that," and I say, "Always, everybody can do everything." You've got to be flexible if you immigrate. It's the most important thing. If you have to do something, you do it.

Ludwig Stern

Germany

I worked up until last year cutting meat. My wife wanted me to stop. I can still do it but it's okay to stop. In life, everything has a beginning and everything has an end. I've done the same kind of work my whole life. Nothing else. My father was a cattle dealer and he had a butcher shop in Germany. I went to school for eight years and then I worked for my father for thirty-eight years. I did everything. It was not too bad. We had a *shochet*, a butcher, for killing kosher.

I met my wife when she was twelve years old. I had my eye on her. I was twenty-five. I wanted to dance with her, but she wouldn't. She said, "Oh, no, I'm too young to dance." A few years later, I met her again at a Chanukah dance and we got married in 1934. She was not as religious as me but I made her religious.

In 1936 or 1937 all of a sudden the Jewish people can do nothing any more—kill no more cattle, buy no more beef. They took all our papers away from us. I went to the synagogue one morning. I took my prayer book and opened the door and the Gestapo came in. They arrested me. I asked them why and they said, "You're Jewish." They asked me some questions and let me out that evening. When I got home I told my wife, "Now is finished." My wife told me she had an uncle in America. I wrote to him and right away he sent the affidavits. We went to the American Consulate with the papers and two weeks later we went on the boat to Manhattan. It was an American boat. The boat ride was very nice. We were in steerage with people who talked English and German.

We stayed in New York for a few days but it was different as night and day when you come from a little town. So many people, and people run around too much, here and there. I said, "We'll go where they have the affidavits." We took the train to Seattle.

I got here Sunday and started working Monday. On Monday I went downtown on the bus but I didn't know you had to pay. The bus driver yells, "Hey, come here!" A man stands up and says, "Where you want to go?" I didn't know the language but then he says, "Sprechen Sie Deutsch?" He says, "You have to pay. I'll pay for you." I say, "I'll look for a job." He says, "I'll show you where to go." He went with me to a packing company where the owner was also from Germany. I tell the owner that I want to start work right away and he tells me to come back in one-half hour. He said, "You'll skin calves." I skinned seven calves for seven dollars. I felt like I'd made a million. I worked there four years.

One afternoon the boss came to me and says, "Ludwig, I forgot the order forms. Go downstairs and pick them up for me in the office." I went down. He took over for me for a minute skinning calves. When I was halfway down the landing, a plane crashed into the building upstairs. A landing piece split my nose. I went running outside and a man says to me, "Ludwig, you saved?" I say, "I think so." I didn't know. I was bleeding and black from gasoline. Forty-one people were killed upstairs, and so was my boss who took my place.

After that, I read in the paper a corned beef maker is wanted. I got the job and made corned beef by thousands of pounds. Then I decided to do it myself. We bought a house that had a butcher shop in the front. I picked up the license and started to work in my own business. I had the best store in town until 1967. Then I gave up my own place and worked here and there, up and down for other people until I was eighty years old. I love being retired. You know what I have to do? Nothing. And I'm not bored at all, not even a little bit, because I love to stay with Mrs. Stern.

Bertha Sulman

Russia

In Russia my mother used to knit socks for the priest who lived across the street from us. It was the highlight of his life. He wouldn't pay any money but he saw to it that nothing should happen to us. It was not so bad. We had chickens, we had a cow, we had vegetables. So we didn't starve.

In about 1906, when I was eight years old, my father and older brother went to America. My father was a shoemaker and it took him a long time to raise enough money to send for us. He and my brother were in Bellingham, Washington. When I was fourteen, he sent for us, my mother and six girls and one boy. We went to Boston first and they detained me and my sister at the immigration station. It was because of our eyes.

My mother had to decide whether to go back to Russia with the whole family or leave my sister and me and go on to Washington. What could she do? When she got to Bellingham, they sent my oldest brother back to Boston to help us. He worked hard and was able to release my sister, but I was kept there.

I was lucky, I guess, because I was young and picked up the language. I learned how to speak English and interpreted for the people. I lived at the immigration station for about a year. I couldn't be with my family so I had to make the best of it. My brother was working the whole time to get me out. In the meantime he met a girl in Boston and got married.

They finally let me go, and I lived with my brother and his new wife for about two years. When I was sixteen, he put me on the train and sent me to Bellingham. It took five days and five nights. When I got to Bellingham, there was a mix-up and nobody met me at the train. They didn't get my mail or something.

I knew I had to get to C Street so I found a bus and asked the driver to take me there. I walked to the address where my mother lived and didn't see nobody there. It was dark and raining. So I went next door and a little girl answered the door. I said, "Do you know where Mrs. Goffee lives?" She said, "Come on, I'll take you to Momma."

It was my little sister. I didn't recognize her. We started running to the house and I saw my mother in the kitchen window. I started yelling, "Momma, Momma, Momma!" They thought I was crazy. I hadn't seen her for three years.

I was always active, always trying. I am still active up to this day. I raised a lot of money for the children in Israel and they still call me to help out at the synagogue. Thank God, our life so far, it couldn't be better. I don't see so good, but I am home with my husband. We have five grandchildren and four great-grandchildren. I have no complaints.

Rose Treiger

Russia

In 1905 my dad thought he'd come to America where he had a brother, and see the opportunities. But what could he do? In Russia we were farmers. He couldn't speak the language so he bought a horse and wagon and started to peddle—junk. He hated every minute of it. In 1907 there was a depression and he couldn't take it, so he went back to Russia. Now that's an unusual thing.

In 1910 my mother said to my father, "Whether you like America or not, I don't want my two sons to serve the czar, so you've got to go back to the United States." So he took my older brother who was reaching the age of eighteen, came back, and again bought a horse and a wagon and peddled. He saved money and in 1911 he sent for us, the family. We arrived in August. I was six and a half. School started in September so I was at the right age of going to first grade. I still have the friends I made that year.

I had two brothers. They started little by little to buy junk with my father. My younger brother used to go around the neighborhood and ask if they had junk to sell. He would leave it on the sidewalk, and my father and older brother would come by and pick it up. That's how we started.

My parents got a little more affluent and they opened a little store in men's clothing. I worked in the store all the time, before school and after school. The odd part of our family is that we never thought "mine and yours." We worked together. I never drew a salary. My brothers never drew a salary. We needed a dollar, we went to the cash register and took it out. Nothing was divided.

I never felt underprivileged in all my life. Now you walk into a kid's bedroom and you see toys in that room—they have more than a store can have, but I never had a doll in my life. I had other things. I had love, I went to school, my mother was always home when we came home. She was not a highly educated woman but she had a lot of common sense, of *sachel*. She knew what was good for us. I know a lot of college graduates today that are not smart at living.

Only in America could we have done all this on our own. Now when I see people that come in as immigrants to America, and they demand everything that we can give them—we never had that sort of thing. I think my father would have been insulted if he had been given something for nothing. He knew he had to work for his living. He made it on his own.

I got married and my husband came into our family business as a bookkeeper. I had two sons. We finally went into business for ourselves. We opened a little general store—a momma and poppa store. They don't have those kind of stores today. For twenty-eight years I used to go to work there morning to night. We had no help. I used to run home when the kids would come home, give them dinner, see that they were making their lessons, and go back to the store until we closed at nine o'clock. Our store was always closed on Saturday, even if it was the day before Christmas.

We did very well: we sent our kids to college.

Today I still keep busy. I love to see people that are living and doing things. I give a lot of book reviews. Every year, once a year, I give a book review for each Jewish organization. I just got done reading a book about the Nazis. I don't want to forget that. My family that didn't come to America was all wiped out when Hitler came into Russia. If it wasn't for my mother's *sachel*, we also would have been wiped out.

Those pictures on the wall are my two sons. Somebody said, "Look, you're not supposed to have pictures like that in the living room. Hang them in your den." I said, "Oh, no, that's my pride and joy." I look at them all the time. Those are *my* dividends.

Irwin Wirth

Germany

My next birthday, I'll be seventy-two. I practice psychiatry in my office three days a week, and still get up at five in the morning. When patients are in the hospital, I see them every day. I owe them that, not to leave them ever unattended. I'm just like the horse that each day finds its way to the stable. It's my routine.

I grew up in a comfortable, very Orthodox home in Würzburg, an old university town, and went to public school there. As a youngster, I went to services with my grandfather three times a day. One of the prayers I still remember very well: "Do not forget the Exodus from Egypt. Those who forget the past may suffer the same anguish in the future."

I went the route of science into medicine. In 1931 I began medical school in Würzburg. The atmosphere at the University became hostile. Lifelong friends joined the Hitler movement and stopped speaking to me. I was two and a half years into medicine, having completed my *Physikum*, my basic sciences, when I decided to leave Germany. I was very fluent in French, so France was the natural place to go, but the French medical school to which I applied would give me only one year of credit for my two and a half years of study. I went instead to Bologna, Italy, in the fall of 1933. Knowing just two words in Italian, yes and no, but having a fair knowledge of Latin at that time, I got an Italian grammar. Within three weeks my papers were translated into Italian and approved by the representative of the Italian Consulate in Munich, I pounded about fifteen hundred words into my head in Italian, went to Rome with my papers, made myself understood, and had two days to register in Bologna.

I graduated from medical school in Bologna in 1937. My father and stepmother had already come to America. I waited till my affidavit from them was in order, spending the interval in Switzerland doing some research, attending courses in Zurich. I came to America in July, 1938. In the winter of 1939 I accepted an internship in Lincoln, Nebraska, and after one and a half years' work there, began a residency in psychiatry at a state hospital in Washington state.

Before World War II broke out, I had applied to the licensing director to take the medical state board examination. I was about to take the exam in the beginning of 1942, and everything was in order. About a week before the exam, however, I received a notice that my permission to take it was revoked because I was an "enemy alien," having been born in Germany.

At this time I was already in my second year of residency.

Shocked and dismayed, I went to the state capitol and spoke to the director of licensing who happened to be hostile to Germans, having been gassed by them during World War I. I finally talked him into allowing me to take the exam. "But," he said, "I do not plan to issue the license right away even if you pass it." I took the exam and received notification that I had passed.

Being an enemy alien, I was curfewed during my second year residency. The Sixth Army Command controlled all enemy alien movements. To go anywhere, I had to have their permission. I could only drive five miles, and only during daylight hours.

The Sixth Army Command eventually transferred their authority to the local police judges. Because the High Holidays were approaching, I sought permission to attend services. An American doctor, my only witness, came with me. The judge had no official forms yet, and simply gave me verbal permission to attend.

Someone denounced me for violating the curfew. The FBI came to investigate. The police judge, fearful of the FBI, denied he had given me permission. As a result, the FBI accused me of being a German spy. "I'm a Jew," I said. "I ran away from Hitler." The response was a threat to intern me as a spy, although they had no evidence.

Eventually the curfew was lifted, but the whole matter put into limbo my application for citizenship. I wanted to vote. It was already my sixth year here. In desperation I went to the U.S. attorney for the Western District. He said, "We'll solve the problem right away." He got the police judge on the phone, who at last admitted he had in fact given me that permission. The next day I was cleared for citizenship.

After all this cleared, I applied for navy service. The army had earlier turned me down because I wasn't a citizen; but for the invasion of Japan, the navy needed an additional fifteen thousand physicians. New Year's morning, 1945, I was examined and cleared for service. Several months later, when I made all my preparations to leave, the first bomb fell in Hiroshima, followed shortly by the bomb on Nagasaki. Within a week's time, I received a telegram from the navy, thanking me for my patriotism. It read: "Because of our victory over Japan, your services will no longer be needed."

Elisabeth Zadek

Germany

We were in Germany and the Nazis, they wouldn't let us live. We were in business until the last moment, 1938, and they put people in front of the store with signs: "Don't Buy from Jews." So we had to sell and we sold it to an old gentile friend of my husband's. He was not a Nazi before, but he became a Nazi and he was very bad. Very bad. And he didn't pay everything he had to pay for the store. Only a little more than half.

Two of our daughters were already in Israel at that time. We had seen it coming. The third daughter stayed with us. Then it became so terrible, and in November 1938, they arrested all the Jewish men in our city, Stettin, and put them in a concentration camp. So was my husband. But at that time, it was the beginning, and they could still get out of the camp with a visa. So I sent a telegram to an uncle of mine who was in Palestine and he sent a visa. With the visa in hand, I went to the Gestapo and said, "Let him free." We had to pay a lot of money to get out.

My husband and daughter and I went to Palestine. We left with a few pieces of furniture so it was not so bad. In Palestine we were there with all my daughters, and we opened a little store. So we lived. But in 1947 the British made us move. They took our part of the city and we all had to get out. They confiscated our store.

They made us move three times. Each time we had to start again. Finally we had a shoe store we kept.

We ended up in America because two of my daughters lived and married here. My husband had become sick and I could not manage the business alone, so we moved to America in 1952. In Israel we lived a normal life with friends. Here in America we had no money and we lived badly. We both worked very hard until the restitution from Germany came. Then, when I was sixty-five, I could live the life I always wished to live. To take care of my husband, to cook, to have a nice home. We had several years that way.

My husband passed away eight years ago. Now I am lonely in my apartment sometimes, but I have my privacy. I have a quiet life, but I am always occupied. I cook, I read, I write letters, I make my crossword puzzles, I go to the museum, I play bridge, I visit my friends, I see my family. I am happy.

Sarah Zetin

Poland

We had a beautiful garden in Poland. I know how to pick flowers, plant carrots, and dig potatoes. I'm a good farmer. And I know how to keep cows in their own field. In Europe the men did nothing but study the Hebrew. My father was a very religious man, and day and night he was reading. My mother went with a big *shaytl*, a headcovering, and everything was strictly kosher. No monkey business.

I liked the way we lived our life, barefoot and with beautiful linen. But we children were compelled to be modern and different from our mothers and fathers. When I was fourteen years old, I came to America with an auntie. My mother didn't want the family to go but I said, "I'll go to America. I'm not afraid." So she let me go with her sister. When we got here, my aunt wouldn't take her eye off me until I was married and had a baby. She saw to it I should have a good husband.

When I was Americanized and my children were nine, twelve, and six years old, my husband and I opened up a store in the public market. It was hard work, but no matter how many hours I spent in the store, my children were always my first concern. It was an Italian grocery store. We had spaghetti, macaroni, cheese, wine, salami, anything what the Italian people want. Ninety-nine percent of the people thought I was Italian. But I cannot and will not deny what I am. If they asked me, I told them. We kept the store closed on Jewish holidays because I'm Jewish and that settles it. I was a good saleslady. If you are honest with people, you get their trade. We had the store twenty-one years.

We made a lot of friends in our store. I always wanted to help people. If a poor man came to me and said he was hungry, then I gave him half of what I had and was satisfied. During the Depression, people had to go and stay in line with a cup to get coffee or something to eat. I was heartbroken, but what could I do? I couldn't give all the people enough to eat. But lots of people would come to our home and knock on the door that they were hungry. My husband said, "Don't let them in, they are liable to kill you." So I had a chain made on the door and when a man said he was hungry, I would give him half of a sandwich through the chain.

Now life is easy, but I'm old. My eyes are tearing, my hearing is poor, I am getting gray. A person changes. It is sometimes tiresome being ninety-seven, but I only hope that when my children grow up they should be as old as I am and feel as good as I do.

The Participants, *Listed Alphabetically by Surname*

Susan Angel, *Turkey*

Regina Avzaradel, *Isle of Rhodes*

Louise Azose, *Turkey*

Annemarie Ballin, *Germany*

Margit Baruch, *Hungary and Austria*

Henry Benezra, *Turkey*

Dona Benoun, *Turkey*

Nicholas Berman, *Hungary*

Z. William Birnbaum, *Poland*

Tamara Birulin, *Russia and China*

Edith Blumenfeld, *Germany*

Joseph Brown (born Bronshtane), *Russia*

Sema Calvo, *Isle of Marmara*

Sol Esfeld, *Poland*

Mitzi Fink, *Czechoslovakia*

John Frankel, *Denmark*

Newman Glass, *Rumania*

Marion Glazer, *Poland*

Ida Goldfine, *Russia*

Daniel Haguel, *Greece*

Goldie Handlin, *Russia*

Arthur Lagawier, *Holland*

Ludwig Lobe, *Germany*

Lucie Loeb, *Switzerland*

Walter Lowen, *Germany*

Sam Bension Maimon, *Turkey*

Sarah Miller, *Russia*

Eric Offenbacher, *Germany*

Albert Ovadia, *Isle of Marmara*

Rachel Peha, *Isle of Rhodes*

Lou Pilisuk, *Austria and Russia*

Harry Policar, *Isle of Marmara*

Hanna Povlsen, *Austria*

Rose Pruzan, *Russia*

Alfred Püchler, *Czechoslovakia*

Leon Rousso, *Isle of Rhodes*

Abraham Sambol, *Poland*

Hazel Saperstein, *Russia*

Max Schoenfeld, *Germany*

Irving Seidman, *Russia*

Jenny Spitzer, *Austria*

Samuel Steinberg, *Russia*

Jeannette Sterling, *Turkey*

Gustave Stern, *Germany*

Ludwig Stern, *Germany*

Bertha Sulman, *Russia*

Rose Treiger, *Russia*

Irwin Wirth, *Germany*

Elisabeth Zadek, *Germany*

Sarah Zetin, *Poland*